"Fighting for Your Prodiga, ⌐ MW01492640   ⊇
for the spirit of heaviness. In curating a year's worth of Bible promises,
Tami Winkelman equips us to pray powerfully and strategically for our
loved ones, even in life's darkest places. This is a book of hope."

Jodie Berndt
Author of *Praying the Scriptures for Your Adult Children*

"What a powerful book! This book was born out of the practical
experience of praying parents, and encourages bold and heartfelt moments
at the throne of grace through Scripture-based promises and prayer-
starters. It also includes praises for each new day—which is so important
for helping you stay focused on our loving Lord as the true Source of help
and strength. Tami Winkelman has forged a vital tool to bless prodigals
and those who love them. My wife and I will use this book to pray for our
prodigal, and look forward to what God will do!"

Dr. James Banks
Author of the best-selling *Prayers for Prodigals*

"Every family, community, and fellowship of believers has their
prodigals—those wandering sheep who have gone astray, not only from
the family but, more so, from the Eternal Father. So, we commit ourselves
to 'stand in the gap' and prayerfully intercede for them. However, as we
battle with demonic powers in the war for lost souls, we can be bombarded
with a spirit of weariness in the fight. Thankfully, Tami Winkelman's
beautiful work, *Fighting for Your Prodigal through Prayer*, is an
inspirational tool of the Holy Spirit to restore our strength. Consequently,
hope and trust in the Shepherd's heart is renewed as the reader is guided
through Bible-based mediation, daily reflections, and prayer directives.
This highly anointed prayer guide is a must for everyone who loves a
prodigal and for those who have passion to intercede and believe that the
drifting child will soon be back in the safe harbor, in the loving arms of
the Father."

Dr. Kenneth Baker

"The prayers and scriptures in this book are an invaluable gift. Tami
has done a wonderful job of providing a powerful collection for moms

and dads of wayward, troubled children. I wish I'd had her book during my daughter's tumultuous years. What a treasure to pick up this book when you don't know how to pray or what Bible verse to turn to. *Fighting for Your Prodigal through Prayer* is perfect for the believing parents who are in the midst of a spiritual battle."

Dena Yohe
Co-founder, Hope for Hurting Parents;
mentor, speaker; award-winning author of
You Are Not Alone: Hope for Hurting Parents of Troubled Kids

"*Fighting for Your Prodigal through Prayer: 365 Promises, Praises, and Prayers* is a book of promises, praises, and prayers that will help you every day. This book will encourage you on your journey to see a prodigal return to right relationship with Christ. It will equip you to fight for the lost son or daughter. I trust you will take time to read each scripture, proclaim the prayers and position yourself for praise. God's promises are true and it's time to declare them over prodigals.

I think you will discover, as I have, that *Fighting for Your Prodigal through Prayer* will change the atmosphere and allow you to do battle against the enemy. Stand firm and see what God is able to do. I agree with you, in Jesus's name, that your *PRODIGAL* is coming home!"

Kevin McGlamery
Lead Pastor, Life Church Huntsville

"You know them—you may even have one in your own family! They're not pariahs, they're prodigals! Jesus gives us the beautiful Parable of the Prodigal in Luke 15, and tells us that restoration is not only possible, but that the returning prodigal should be celebrated! Jesus is intent on bringing your prodigal home. 'What man of you, having an hundred sheep, if he lose one of them, doth not leave the ninety and nine in the wilderness, and go after that which is lost, until he find it?' (Luke 15:4 KJV). Can you imagine the prayers that the prodigal's father prayed? This incredible book will help you envision and put into action those prayers. I've observed the life of the author of this ingenious primer as she has labored in prayer over her own 'prodigal.' Her love and devotion was only matched by her ardent and passionate prayer. That passion fueled her desire to help others in the painful but joyous process of praying for prodigals. You hold in your hands one of the best actionable sources to help motivate your own prodigal to begin the trek homeward. You may discover something about yourself as you pray your prodigal back to Him!"

Rev. James R. Bond
Senior Pastor, Revival Tabernacle

"*Fighting for Your Prodigal through Prayer* is a Wonderful resource to add to your spiritual arsenal that includes: *Word, Witness and Warrior. Word*—there is no substitute for the Word of God. This resource offers the biblical principles guiding your prayers. You are praying the Word of God. Praying with the Word of God leads to the Will of God. *Witness*—each prayer offers a change in focus from our frustration to His faith (promise). That change in focus will change our testimony (Witness). *Warrior*—as you use this resource, you may feel you are praying as a spiritual 'mama bear' fighting for your loved one. If you are at a place of not knowing what to do or how to pray, this resource will be a great help. Your prayers are not just changing now, but eternity."

Dr. H. E. Cardin
Lead Pastor, Bellshire Ministries;
Lee University Adjunct; Pentecostal Theological Seminary Adjunct

"When you love a prodigal, you keep loving, pursuing, correcting— you try everything you can think of to bring him back, restore her, save their lives. And you pray. Yet even then you need help: What to pray? How to trust God? How to not give up? Good news: Tami Winkelman has provided the help you need. Her book is scriptural, practical and full of love, grace, faith and hope. She will get you started in believing prayer— and God will carry you the rest of the way."

Judy Douglass
Founder, Worldwide Prodigal Prayer Day and author of
When You Love a Prodigal: 90 Days of Grace for the Wilderness
founder, Prayer for Prodigals online community

Fighting

for Your

Prodigal

through

Prayer

Fighting

for Your

Prodigal

through

Prayer

365 Promises, Praises, and Prayers

Tami Winkelman

To all those who pray for and love a prodigal
that you will rest in God's promises
and soon see your prodigal once again saved and
loving and serving God.

TABLE OF CONTENTS

ACKNOWLEDGMENTS

To my incredible husband, Kevin: thank you for always supporting, consulting, loving, believing, helping, and praying, and for walking this ministry with me. My words are not sufficient to express my gratitude and love for you.

To my children: Taylor, thank you for graciously cheering me on. Evin, thank you for supporting, listening, and always believing in this ministry and lending technical support. I always pray for God's best for you both.

To my parents, Pastor A. L. and Carol Henderson: thank you for praying, encouraging, and always believing and all the other ways you've helped me in life and the writing of this book.

To Erin Swinford: thank you for partnering with me in starting a Prayer for Prodigals group at Life Church Huntsville seven years ago. God has saved 37 prodigals so far with many more to come!

To the Life Church Huntsville Prayer for Prodigals team: thank you for always praying, supporting, checking in, and ministering with me. You are incredible, and I am honored to pray in agreement with you.

To Rita: thank you for being my prayer partner for prodigals you don't even know.

To Joyce: thank you for going around the mountain with me until....

To Whitney: thank you for unreserved editorial and formatting support.

To those who read chapters for clarity, those who gave theological advice, and those who loved me through the process: I am grateful for you all.

FIRST THINGS FIRST

Prayer changes things. You have probably heard this from a pulpit or read it on a bumper sticker. The saying may have become so commonplace that its effect on you has diminished, or you may not have witnessed many answered prayers for your prodigal, but this truth never diminishes. Prayer is the only hope for the salvation of your son or daughter who has left relationship with the Lord: your prodigal. Satan definitely is not going to give them up without a fight, and the best way to fight is on your knees.

You most likely picked up this book because you love a prodigal and desperately desire to see him or her saved, serving God, and on the pathway to heaven. Possibly, despite heroic effort, you realize you cannot force salvation into his or her heart and that prayer is the only true way to bring about the heart changes you long to see. God is the answer. He is the only One who can draw prodigals back to Himself.

Since God will not force salvation on anyone, and since we cannot manipulate God through our prayers no matter how perfect they are, what good does prayer do? It does so much good! In answer to your prayer, God will create conditions that free your prodigal to make a decision for Him.

In answer to prayer, God will

- Replace a heart of stone with a heart of flesh (Ezekiel 36:26).
- Lift the veil and open their eyes and ears to the truth (Isaiah 35:5; Psalm 146:8).

- Put godly people in their pathway (Matthew 9:38; 2 Timothy 2:25–26).
- Remove ungodly influences (Psalm 140:4).
- Cause them to come to their senses (2 Timothy 2:25–26; Acts 26:18; Isaiah 42:7).
- Hedge them in to keep them away from evil and to keep evil from them (Psalm 139:5; Hosea 2:6; 1 Chronicles 4:10).
- Cause them to detest the sin in their lives (Proverbs 8:13; Jude 15–16).
- Expose lies of Satan as lies (John 8:32).
- Heal a hurt (Isaiah 57:18).
- Tear down strongholds (2 Corinthians 10:5; Romans 6:14).
- Send angels to fight for them (Hebrews 1:14).
- Illuminate the dark places in their lives (Acts 26:18).
- Block a path they need to avoid (Proverbs 16:9; Hosea 2:6).
- Hear their cry (Psalm 107:28).
- Deliver them from addiction (John 8:36; Psalm 146:7; Isaiah 61:1; Romans 6:14).

HE WILL SET THEM UP TO RECEIVE SALVATION!

A Few Foundational Verses to Get Us Started

An army of one million headed to Judah to fight against King Asa's army of 580,000; they were outnumbered almost two to one. "And Asa cried out to the LORD his God, and said, 'LORD, it is nothing for You to help, whether with many or with those who have no power; help us, O LORD our God, for we rest on You, and in Your name we go against this multitude. O LORD, You are our God; do not let man prevail against You!'" (2 Chronicles 14:11 NKJV). Read further and you will find that God defeated the million-man army and gave the spoil to Judah. Then He gave the surrounding cities into their hands also, and they carried away their spoil too!

It doesn't matter how bad the situation looks with your prodigal, whether he or she has a few hang-ups or many, is a good person, or is wracked with evil, God is able! And I believe He will also save the prodigal's friends (the spoils from the other cities) too!

One of my favorite verses to pray is Philippians 1:6: "being confident of this very thing, that He who has begun a good work in you will complete it until the day of Jesus Christ." If you have been praying, and I am sure you have, God has already begun a good work, and He *is* able to complete it! What seems hard to us, difficult to us, impossible to us, is not to God. He is God Almighty, sovereign God, omnipotent God. Never underestimate the God who created your prodigal. Trust Him. He's got them. He's working when we can and cannot see it.

How to Use This Book

This book contains 365 prayer starters divided by calendar dates into themed months.

The format of the prayer starters includes:

Promise: Scripture which pertains to either prayer or to His plans for prodigals. Thank God for the promise, then use it to begin entering His gates with thanksgiving, as the Bible instructs in Psalm 100:4. Tell Him of your gratitude for the things He has already done, is doing, and has promised to do in your prodigal's life.

Praise: A name or attribute of God, sometimes accompanied by Scripture, which reveals His ability or propensity to answer the scriptural prayer that follows. Allow this praise time to build your faith as you worship God for who He is and what He can do.

Prayer: A scriptural prayer starter which helps you to pray in God's perfect will for your prodigal that usually begins with *Our Father*, as Jesus instructed in Matthew 6:9, and includes *in Jesus's name* (John 14:13, 15:16, 16:23). No a*men* is included to encourage you to continue to pour out your heart to God in your prodigal's behalf.

If you are beginning this book in the middle of the year, jump in anyway. Put check marks by the days you pray so when your prodigal is saved, he or she can see God's faithfulness to answer prayer and your love that caused you to pray. When God gives you a raindrop—evidence He is answering your prayers—document it on the "My Raindrops" pages in the back of the book along with the date. (See "April:

Raindrops" for further description.) Rejoice over these raindrops, these evidences that God has begun a good work toward the salvation of your prodigal.

When you need a personal encouragement, read the verses in Appendix A, and ask God to help your unbelief as the child's father did in Mark 9:24.

When you face specific situations with your prodigal and need prayers for those circumstances, check Appendix B for categorized scriptural prayers. Both appendices can help you get through tough times.

As you pray through the book, highlight promises or prayers that speak to you so you can return to them easily.

There is comfort in knowing so many people will be coming against Satan's schemes in the same way each day. There is power in agreement. Put your prodigal where he or she needs to be, in God's hands every day, and go about your business and fulfill your calling in ministry. Pray without ceasing as Paul instructed in 1 Thessalonians 5:17, but do not let this season in the life of your prodigal paralyze you, spiritually or functionally. Praying without ceasing is having knee time every day, praying flash prayers as the Spirit leads, and never giving up.

When your prodigal is saved, please, continue praying these prayer starters over someone else's prodigal, and write me so I may rejoice with you! (prayerforprodigals7@gmail.com)

Praying Individually or in a Group

> "Again I say unto you, That if two of you shall agree on earth as touching any thing that they shall ask, it shall be done for them of my Father which is in heaven. For where two or three are gathered together in my name, there am I in the midst of them" (Matthew 18:19–20 KJV).

If possible, find others to pray with you.

There is power in agreement in prayer. When, where, and how long to pray is up to you. I suggest keeping a list of prodigals for whom to pray and a list of those saved. I also suggest that prayer during this time be solely for the salvation of prodigals. It is easy to get distracted and burdened for so many other needs. When people find out you meet to pray, they will ask for their prayer needs as well. There is a time and place for praying for other needs. It is also a good idea that food not become a part of the meeting. Once again, this distracts from the real purpose.

Some Things to Remember While Praying for Your Prodigal

- We do not have to be afraid.
- We CAN touch Almighty God for our prodigals as we mind the gap between them and God.
- There are promises in God's word that we can take to the bank.
- God has this; He is faithful; we can trust Him.
- We walk in victory while praying through circumstances, knowing those circumstances do not change the promises of God.
- God sometimes gives us evidence of answered prayers for prodigals, and our faith increases as we thank God.
- God loves our prodigals more than we do, and He wants them saved and living for Him more than we do.
- While there is not a perfect formula to pray to God to make Him save prodigals when we want Him to, nor a foolproof method designed to force God to keep our interpretation of His promises, we *can* take Him at His word, knowing that what He has promised He will do.
- God's process is much more effective than ours. He is smarter than us, and He is stronger than us.
- When God looks at our prodigals, He sees something different from what we see. Yes, He knows right where they are in this moment, but He also sees them as they will be. We may see bad decisions, bad health, arrogance, lack of faith,

but God sees how they can be. The world may say they are dead, but God says He sees life in them!

- God will do His part. Our part is to love our prodigals unconditionally and to obey God: in prayer, praying His word back to Him; in fasting, not manipulating God, but putting ourselves in a place where we can hear Him clearly and will obey more readily; and fulfilling our calling and purpose, as well as anything else He asks us to do.

Like Nehemiah said to those returned from captivity, let me say to you: "Do not be afraid of them. Remember the Lord, great and awesome, and fight for your brethren, your sons, your daughters, your wives, and your houses" (Nehemiah 4:14).

Never give up! Keep praying! Prayer really does change things!

JANUARY

DO NOT BE AFRAID

"Be not afraid, only believe" (Mark 5:36 KJV).

In Mark 5:22-42 we find the story of a ruler of the synagogue, Jairus, seeking healing from Jesus for his little girl. He fell at Jesus's feet and begged Him, so Jesus agreed to go with Jairus to his house.

On the way, Jesus was delayed by the woman who touched the hem of His garment, and while He talked to her, "some came from the ruler of the synagogue's house who said, 'Your daughter is dead. Why trouble the Teacher any further?'" (verse 35).

Does this sound familiar? Does Satan lie to you saying there is no need to pray, your prodigal is too far gone away from God, he or she can never be saved, he or she is too dead to live again, or you are wasting your time when you talk to God for him or her?

When Jesus heard the proclamation of death, He said to Jairus, "Do not be afraid; only believe" (verse 36).

We've prayed. We've invited God to work in the lives of our prodigals. When our faith is low, we must remember those words of Jesus: "Do not be afraid; only believe."

What happened with Jairus' daughter? When Jesus arrived at Jairus' house, He found a commotion of mourning, as one would expect with the death of a child. But Jesus said, "Why make this commotion and weep?" (verse 39). It *seemed* the child had died. From every external evidence, the little girl was dead, but Jesus knew the truth.

Why do we trouble ourselves and fret when our heavenly Father is on the job? It may seem our prodigal is dead—all evidence may point to that conclusion—but when He gives us a promise, we can rest knowing He knows the truth, that there is life.

We know what He did next. He told the little girl to arise, and *she did*!

I believe the Lord wants to say that to all of our prodigals: "ARISE! Come back to life!"

And when He tells them to arise, they will! But in the meantime, why make any commotion and weep? Don't be afraid. Just believe!

1. PROMISE: "You shall not be terrified of them; for the LORD your God, the great and awesome God, is among you" (Deuteronomy 7:21).

   PRAISE: Jehovah Nissi, The Lord Our Banner—Nissi is also translated ensign or standard.

   PRAYER: Our Father, I ask You to help _____. Be his/her refuge. Keep Your everlasting arms underneath him/her and throw the enemy out from before him/her, and say, "Destroy them" (Deuteronomy 33:27 KJV). In Jesus's name I pray.

2. PROMISE: "When you go out to battle against your enemies, and see horses and chariots and people more numerous than you, do not be afraid of them; for the LORD your God is with you, who brought you up from the land of Egypt" (Deuteronomy 20:1).

   PRAISE: Omnipotent, all-powerful

   PRAYER: Our Father, in Jesus's name I ask You to preserve _____'s going out and coming in from now and forevermore (Psalm 121:8).

3. PROMISE: "Be strong and of good courage, do not fear nor be afraid of them; for the LORD your God, He is the One who goes with you. He will not leave you nor forsake you" (Deuteronomy 31:6).

    PRAISE: Jehovah Nissi, The Lord Our Banner—"When the enemy shall come in like a flood, the Spirit of the LORD shall lift up a standard against him" (Isaiah 59:19 KJV).

    PRAYER: Our Father, _____ is desolate and afflicted and his/her heart troubles are growing larger. Please have mercy on my prodigal, bring him/her out of distress, and forgive his/her sins (Psalm 25:16–18 KJV). I pray this in Jesus's name.

4. PROMISE: "And the LORD, He is the One who goes before you. He will be with you, He will not leave you nor forsake you; do not fear nor be dismayed" (Deuteronomy 31:8).

    PRAISE: Shield

    PRAYER: Our Father, I pray in Jesus's name that You do not deliver _____ to his/her enemies' will (Psalm 27:12).

5. PROMISE: "The LORD is my light and my salvation; whom shall I fear? the LORD is the strength of my life; of whom shall I be afraid?" (Psalm 27:1 KJV).

    PRAISE: Savior and Defense

    PRAYER: Our Father, I ask in Jesus's name that _____ will know his/her salvation comes from You and that You are his/her rock and defense (Psalm 62:1–2).

6. PROMISE: "I had fainted, unless I had believed to see the goodness of the LORD in the land of the living" (Psalm 27:13 KJV).

   PRAISE: Good

   PRAYER: Our Father, cause _____ to seek good and not evil, so he/she may live and You will be with him/her (Amos 5:14). I pray in the name of Jesus.

7. PROMISE: "Wait on the LORD; Be of good courage, And He shall strengthen your heart; Wait, I say, on the LORD!" (Psalm 27:14).

   PRAISE: "And in that day you will say: 'Praise the LORD, call upon His name; Declare His deeds among the peoples, Make mention that His name is exalted'" (Isaiah 12:4).

   PRAYER: Our Father, I am waiting to see _____ saved, and I thank You for strengthening my heart while I wait. I pray in Jesus's name that my prodigal will come to You so he/she will not be cast out (John 6:37).

8. PROMISE: "I sought the LORD, and he heard me, and delivered me from all my fears" (Psalm 34:4 KJV).

   PRAISE: Deliverer

   PRAYER: Our Father, in Jesus's name I pray that _____ will seek You, and that You will hear him/her and deliver my prodigal from all his/her fears.

9. PROMISE: "By awesome deeds in righteousness You will answer us, O God of our salvation, You who are the confidence of all the ends of the earth, And of the far-off seas" (Psalm 65:5).

PRAISE: Jehovah Shammah, The Lord Is There

PRAYER: Our Father, when _____ calls on You, answer him/her; be with him/her in trouble, and deliver him/her (Psalm 91:15). I pray in Jesus's name.

10. PROMISE: "And he shall say to them, 'Hear, O Israel: Today you are on the verge of battle with your enemies. Do not let your heart faint, do not be afraid, and do not tremble or be terrified because of them; for the LORD your God is He who goes with you, to fight for you against your enemies, to save you'" (Deuteronomy 20:3–4).

PRAISE: El-Shaddai, The Almighty, All-Sufficient God

PRAYER: Our Father, I ask You to preserve _____ from violent men, who have purposed to make his/her steps stumble (Psalm 140:4). In Jesus's name I pray.

11. PROMISE: "The LORD has made known His salvation; His righteousness He has revealed in the sight of the nations" (Psalm 98:2).

PRAISE: Revealer

PRAYER: Our Father, I pray that _____ will be led by the Spirit of God and be Your son/daughter in Jesus's name (Romans 8:14).

12. PROMISE: "He will not always strive with us, Nor will He keep His anger forever" (Psalm 103:9).

    PRAISE: Longsuffering

    PRAYER: Our Father, I ask in Jesus's name that You do not let _____ die for lack of instruction or go astray in the greatness of his/her folly (Proverbs 5:23).

13. PROMISE: "Behold, God is my salvation; I will trust, and not be afraid: for the LORD JEHOVAH is my strength and my song; he also is become my salvation" (Isaiah 12:2 KJV).

    PRAISE: Strength and Song

    PRAYER: Our Father, in Jesus's name I pray that _____ will receive Your salvation, trust You, and not be afraid. Please be _____'s strength and song.

14. PROMISE: "He has not dealt with us according to our sins, Nor punished us according to our iniquities" (Psalm 103:10).

    PRAISE: Counselor

    PRAYER: Our Father, I ask You to direct _____'s steps by Your word, and do not let iniquity dominate him/her (Psalm 119:133). I pray this in Jesus's name.

15. PROMISE: "The righteous will be in everlasting remembrance. He will not be afraid of evil tidings; His heart is steadfast, trusting in the LORD. His heart is established; He will not be afraid, Until he sees his desire upon his enemies" (Psalm 112:6–8).

PRAISE: Faithful

PRAYER: Our Father, I ask in Jesus's name that You will cause _____ to trust in You with all his/her heart: and lean not unto his/her own understanding (Proverbs 3:5 KJV).

16. PROMISE: "Who shall bring a charge against God's elect? It is God who justifies" (Romans 8:33).

PRAISE: Deliverer

PRAYER: Our Father, please deliver _____ from those whose ways are crooked (Proverbs 2:15 KJV). In Jesus's name I pray.

17. PROMISE: "Peace I leave with you, My peace I give to you; not as the world gives do I give to you. Let not your heart be troubled, neither let it be afraid" (John 14:27).

PRAISE: Jehovah M'Kaddesh, The Lord Who Sanctifies

PRAYER: God of peace, sanctify _____ completely. I pray that his/her body, soul, and spirit be preserved blameless unto the coming of our Lord Jesus Christ (1 Thessalonians 5:23 KJV). I ask these things in Jesus's name.

18. PROMISE: "In the fear of the LORD is strong confidence: and his children shall have a place of refuge" (Proverbs 14:26 KJV).

PRAISE: Defender

PRAYER: Our Father, bring our sons and daughters back to You (Isaiah 43:6). Place a hedge of thorns and a wall around

_____ so he/she will no longer walk the sinful paths. When he/she seeks sin, do not let him/her find it. Cause _____ to say, "I will go and return to [the Lord], For then it was better for me than now" (Hosea 2:7). I ask these things in Jesus's name.

19. PROMISE: "Do not fear, nor be afraid; Have I not told you from that time, and declared it? You are My witnesses. Is there a God besides Me? Indeed there is no other Rock; I know not one" (Isaiah 44:8).

PRAISE: El Elyon, God Most High

PRAYER: Our Father, I pray in Jesus's name that _____ will beware of false prophets, which come in sheep's clothing, but inwardly they are ravening wolves (Matthew 7:15 KJV).

20. PROMISE: "Whenever I am afraid, I will trust in You" (Psalm 56:3).

PRAISE: Jehovah Raah, The Lord Our Shepherd

PRAYER: Our Father, _____ has gone astray like a lost sheep. Seek him/her. Save him/her. Bring back our captivity, O Lord, in Jesus's name (Psalm 119:176; 126:4).

21. PROMISE: "But now, thus says the LORD, who created you, O Jacob, And He who formed you, O Israel: 'Fear not, for I have redeemed you; I have called you by your name; you are Mine. When you pass through the waters, I will be with you; And through the rivers, they shall not overflow you. When you walk through the fire, you shall not be burned, Nor shall the flame scorch you'" (Isaiah 43:1–2).

PRAISE: Redeemer

PRAYER: Our Father, I pray in Jesus's name that _____ would walk worthy of You, the One who has called him/her into Your own kingdom and glory (1 Thessalonians 2:12).

22. PROMISE: "Be not afraid, only believe" (Mark 5:36 KJV).

PRAISE: Revealer

PRAYER: Our Father, I ask You to tell _____ to rise up and live again in You (Mark 5:41). In Jesus's name I pray.

23. PROMISE: "Launch out into the deep and let down your nets for a catch" (Luke 5:4). "Do not be afraid. From now on you will catch men" (Luke 5:10). "I am willing; be cleansed" (Luke 5:13).

PRAISE: Sovereign

PRAYER: Our Father, in these words of Jesus I find promise and hope, and although You do not force anyone to be saved, I pray in Jesus's name and according to Your word that You will set_____ up to receive salvation.
- Send laborers into the harvest field (Matthew 9:38).
- Replace ungodly influences with godly ones (Psalm 1:1).
- Help him/her take the way of escape when he/she is tempted to sin (1 Corinthians 10:13).
- Remove _____'s heart of stone and give him/her a heart of flesh (Ezekiel 11:19).
- Convict him/her of sin (John 16:8).
- Draw _____ to Yourself (John 6:44).

24. PROMISE: "Fear not, little flock; for it is your Father's good pleasure to give you the kingdom" (Luke 12:32 KJV).

PRAISE: Father

PRAYER: Our Father, thank You for this promise. I pray _____ will call on Your name and be saved. It is my heart's desire that he/she be part of Your kingdom. I ask this in Jesus's name.

25. PROMISE: "Let not your heart be troubled; you believe in God, believe also in Me" (John 14:1).

PRAISE: Adonai, Lord and Master

PRAYER: Our Father, I pray in Jesus's name that _____ will believe in You and Your Son.

26. PROMISE: "Peace I leave with you, My peace I give to you; not as the world gives do I give to you. Let not your heart be troubled, neither let it be afraid" (Jesus in John 14:27).

PRAISE: Jehovah Shalom, The Lord Our Peace

PRAYER: Our Father, help me to rest in the peace that comes from knowing Your promises and trusting in them. I pray in Jesus's name that _____ will depart from evil, and do good; seek peace, and pursue it (Psalm 34:14).

27. PROMISE: "And Paul went down, and fell on him, and embracing him said, Trouble not yourselves; for his life is in him" (Acts 20:10 KJV).

PRAISE: Life

PRAYER: Our Father, Paul knew there was life in Eutychus when others thought he was dead, and there is life in _____. I see the promise of that life and ask You to raise _____ up from spiritual death. In Jesus's name I pray.

28. PROMISE: "For God has not given us a spirit of fear, but of power and of love and of a sound mind" (2 Timothy 1:7).

PRAISE: Omnipotent, all-powerful God

PRAYER: Our Father, I ask that _____ will stir up Your gift which is in him/her, because You have not given him/her a spirit of fear, but of power, love, and a sound mind (2 Timothy 1:6–7). I pray in Jesus's name.

29. PROMISE: "And I will gather the remnant of my flock out of all countries whither I have driven them, and will bring them again to their folds; and they shall be fruitful and increase. And I will set up shepherds over them which shall feed them: and they shall fear no more, nor be dismayed, neither shall they be lacking, saith the LORD" (Jeremiah 23:3–4 KJV).

PRAISE: Jehovah Raah, The Lord Our Shepherd

PRAYER: Our Father, I ask that You will bring _____ back to Your fold, and that he/she will be fruitful and increase. Please, provide shepherds who will feed him/her. Cause him/her to not fear, be dismayed, or lack. I pray this in Jesus's name.

30. PROMISE: "For I am not ashamed of the gospel of Christ, for it is the power of God to salvation for everyone who believes, for the Jew first and also for the Greek" (Romans 1:16).

PRAISE: Jehovah M'Kaddesh, The Lord Who Sanctifies

PRAYER: Our Father, in Jesus's name I pray that _____ will be clean, cease to do evil, and learn to do good (Isaiah 1:16–17).

31. PROMISE: "You are of God, little children, and have overcome them, because He who is in you is greater than he who is in the world" (1 John 4:4).

PRAISE: El, God Of Power And Might

PRAYER: Our Father, Satan desires to sift _____ as wheat, but like Jesus prayed for Simon, I pray that _____'s faith will not fail, and that when he/she has returned to You, he/she will strengthen others (Luke 22:31–32). In Jesus's name I pray.

PRAY–ER ENCOURAGEMENT: The natural reactions to some situations in the lives of our prodigals is fear, causing a commotion, or crying because of lack of hope. Those are natural reactions, but neither of these reactions is necessary because we have committed our prodigal to God in prayer this month while learning to trust Him more. When you feel a natural reaction starting, let the spiritual reaction take over, and trust.

FEBRUARY

"WHO TOUCHED ME?"

Someone touched Jesus without asking permission. Someone had been healed, because Jesus felt the power leave Himself.

"Now a woman, having a flow of blood for twelve years, who had spent all her livelihood on physicians and could not be healed by any, came from behind and *touched the border of His garment*. And immediately her flow of blood stopped. And Jesus said, 'Who touched Me?' When all denied it, Peter and those with him said, 'Master, the multitudes throng and press You, and You say, "Who touched Me?"' But Jesus said, 'Somebody touched Me, *for I perceived power going out from Me.*' Now when the woman saw that she was not hidden, she came trembling; and falling down before Him, *she declared to Him in the presence of all the people the reason she had touched Him and how she was healed immediately.* And He said to her, 'Daughter, be of good cheer; *your faith has made you well. Go in peace*'" (Luke 8:43–48, emphasis added).

This historical story tells us some significant things:

1. Just a touch can do the work of healing; He is such a powerful God.
2. A touch can cause the power of God to be released.
3. When our prodigals are saved, we are to declare publicly what God has done!
4. Our faith makes the difference. If you lack faith, ask God to help your unbelief (Mark 9:24).

19

We are touching the Lord, seeking the Lord, crying and calling out to God, praying Scriptures, setting up banners, and claiming promises for our prodigals, and it is making a difference.

By the way, we NEVER have to ask Jesus's permission before touching Him for our prodigals. We have a standing invitation. In John 14:14, Jesus says, "If you ask anything in My name, I will do it," and in Hebrews 4:16, we are told, "Let us therefore come boldly unto the throne of grace, that we may obtain mercy, and find grace to help in time of need" (KJV).

1. PROMISE: "And Jesus, immediately knowing in himself that virtue had gone out of him, turned him about in the press, and said, Who touched my clothes?" (Mark 5:30 KJV).

   PRAISE: El, God Of Power And Might

   PRAYER: Our Father, I am reaching out and touching You for _____. Send forth the Spirit of Your Son into _____'s heart and cause him/her to cry out, "Abba, Father!" (Galatians 4:6). I pray this in Jesus's name.

2. PROMISE: "The young lions do lack and suffer hunger: but they that seek the LORD shall not want any good thing" (Psalm 34:10 KJV).

   PRAISE: Jehovah Tsidkenu, The Lord Our Righteousness

   PRAYER: Our Father, may _____ hunger and thirst after righteousness, for he/she shall be filled and blessed (Matthew 5:6). I pray this in Jesus's name.

3. PROMISE: "We will rejoice in your salvation, And in the name of our God we will set up our banners!" (Psalm 20:5).

PRAISE: Jehovah Nissi, The Lord Our Banner

PRAYER: Our Father, Your word says, "Neither is there salvation in any other: for there is none other name under heaven given among men, whereby we must be saved" (Acts 4:12 KJV). I pray _____ would trust Your name and be saved, delivered from any strongholds, healed of any hurts, and rescued and protected from any plans Satan has to steal, kill, or destroy him/her. Stake Your banner in _____ in Jesus's name.

4. PROMISE: "For You, Lord, are good, and ready to forgive, And abundant in mercy to all those who call upon You" (Psalm 86:5).

    PRAISE: Merciful

    PRAYER: "O Lord, hear! O Lord, forgive! O Lord, listen and act! Do not delay for Your own sake, my God" (Daniel 9:19). I pray this in Jesus's name.

5. PROMISE: "He will regard the prayer of the destitute, and not despise their prayer. This shall be written for the generation to come: and the people which shall be created shall praise the LORD" (Psalm 102:17–18 KJV).

    PRAISE: Life—"The thief does not come except to steal, and to kill, and to destroy. I have come that they may have life, and that they may have it more abundantly" (John 10:10).

    PRAYER: Our Father, sometimes I feel destitute because of the life lived by my prodigal, but I know You do not despise my prayers for _____. Please, show him/her that a way that seems right to a man is the way of death (Proverbs 14:12). Cause him/her to choose the way of life. I pray this in Jesus's name.

6. PROMISE: "For He looked down from the height of His sanctuary; From heaven the LORD viewed the earth, To hear the groaning of the prisoner, To release those appointed to death" (Psalm 102:19–20).

   PRAISE: Deliverer

   PRAYER: Our Father, thank You for this promise! Make _____ free from the law of sin and death (Romans 8:2). I pray this in Jesus's name.

7. PROMISE: "He who covers his sins will not prosper, But whoever confesses and forsakes them will have mercy" (Proverbs 28:13).

   PRAISE: Merciful

   PRAYER: Our Father, I pray that _____ will not cover his/her sins but will confess and forsake them, so that he/she will have mercy from You. I pray this in Jesus's name.

8. PROMISE: "Therefore with joy you will draw water From the wells of salvation" (Isaiah 12:3).

   PRAISE: Jehovah Raah, The Lord Our Shepherd

   PRAYER: Our Father, this is a wonderful promise! I believe I will celebrate with joy because of _____'s salvation! Cause him/her to "lie down in green pastures," and lead him/her "beside the still waters." Restore his/her soul (Psalm 23:2–3 KJV). I pray this in Jesus's name.

9. PROMISE: "For He says: 'In an acceptable time I have heard you, And in the day of salvation I have helped you.' Behold, now is the accepted time; behold, now is the day of salvation" (2 Corinthians 6:2).

    PRAISE: Savior

    PRAYER: Our Father, I know it is not Your will for anyone to sin; I know it is Your perfect will that all come to repentance (2 Peter 3:9). I pray You will give _____ the shield of Your salvation and hold him/her up with Your right hand (Psalm 18:35). I pray this in Jesus's name.

10. PROMISE: "And you will seek Me and find Me, when you search for Me with all your heart" (Jeremiah 29:13).

    PRAISE: Jehovah Shammah, The Lord Is There

    PRAYER: Our Father, I ask that _____ will pray and seek Your face, and turn from his/her wicked ways, and that You will hear him/her and forgive his/her sin and heal his/her land (2 Chronicles 7:14). I pray this in Jesus's name.

11. PROMISE: "Then you will call upon Me and go and pray to Me, and I will listen to you" (Jeremiah 29:12).

    PRAISE: El Roi, The God Who Sees Me

    PRAYER: Our Father, thank You for always listening to my prayers for _____. I pray that he/she will call on You from his/her place of captivity. When he/she does, thank You for listening and answering. I pray this in Jesus's name.

12. PROMISE: "Again I say unto you, That if two of you shall agree on earth as touching any thing that they shall ask, it shall be done for them of my Father which is in heaven. For where two or three are gathered together in my name, there am I in the midst of them" (Matthew 18:19–20 KJV).

   PRAISE: Savior

   PRAYER: Our Father, thank You for hearing and answering my prayers for _____. "Save now, I pray, O Lord; O Lord, I pray, send now prosperity" (Psalm 118:25). I ask this in Jesus's name.

13. PROMISE: "No more shall every man teach his neighbor, and every man his brother, saying, 'Know the Lord,' for they all shall know Me, from the least of them to the greatest of them, says the Lord. For I will forgive their iniquity, and their sin I will remember no more" (Jeremiah 31:34).

   PRAISE: Jehovah Tsidkenu, The Lord Our Righteousness

   PRAYER: Our Father, in Jesus's name I claim this promise for _____, that he/she will know You, and that You will forgive his/her iniquity, and remember his/her sin no more.

14. PROMISE: "When I cry out to You, Then my enemies will turn back; This I know, because God is for me" (Psalm 56:9).

   PRAISE: Jehovah Nissi, The Lord Our Banner

   PRAYER: Our Father, deliver _____ according to Your word (Psalm 119:170). I pray this in Jesus's name.

15. PROMISE: "And it shall come to pass That whoever calls on the name of the LORD Shall be saved" (Joel 2:32).

    PRAISE: Savior

    PRAYER: Our Father, I am asking that _____ will call upon Your name, and that You save him/her when he/she prays (Acts 2:21). I pray this in Jesus's name.

16. PROMISE: "Ask, and you will receive, that your joy may be full" (John 16:24).

    PRAISE: Redeemer

    PRAYER: Our Father, You promised that if I ask, I will receive. I ask that _____ will "be saved, and ... come unto the knowledge of the truth" (1 Timothy 2:4 KJV). Please restore salvation's joy to him/her. I pray this in Jesus's name.

17. PROMISE: "Now to Him who is able to do exceedingly abundantly above all that we ask or think, according to the power that works in us" (Ephesians 3:20).

    PRAISE: Able

    PRAYER: Our Father, You are able, so please do exceedingly abundantly above all that we even ask or think in _____'s life. I pray this in Jesus's name.

18. PROMISE: "Seeing then that we have a great high priest, that is passed into the heavens, Jesus the Son of God, let us hold fast our profession. For we have not a high priest which cannot be touched with the feeling of our infirmities; but was in all points

tempted like as we are, yet without sin. Let us therefore come boldly unto the throne of grace, that we may obtain mercy, and find grace to help in time of need" (Hebrews 4:14–16 KJV).

PRAISE: High Priest

PRAYER: Our Father, Jesus can sympathize with our weaknesses, so I pray that _____ will feel free to boldly come to Your throne of grace, and that You will grant mercy and grace in his/her time of need.

19. PROMISE: "Thus says the LORD: 'Refrain your voice from weeping, And your eyes from tears; For your work shall be rewarded, says the LORD, And they shall come back from the land of the enemy'" (Jeremiah 31:16).

PRAISE: Faithful

PRAYER: Our Father, just like the prodigal son "came to himself" (Luke 15:17), cause _____ to come to himself/herself and return to You. I pray this in Jesus's name.

20. PROMISE: "Submit yourselves therefore to God. Resist the devil, and he will flee from you" (James 4:7 KJV).

PRAISE: Defense

PRAYER: Our Father, thank You for this promise. I pray _____ will submit to You and resist the devil in Jesus's name.

21. PROMISE: "And if any man sin, we have an advocate with the Father, Jesus Christ the righteous" (1 John 2:1 KJV).

PRAISE: Advocate

PRAYER: Our Father, cause _____ to come to himself/herself in his/her place of captivity and repent and admit he/she has done wrong. When he/she repents, forgive him/her (1 Kings 8:47, 50). I pray this in Jesus's name.

22. PROMISE: "And you shall know the truth, and the truth shall make you free. … Therefore, if the Son makes you free, you shall be free indeed" (John 8:32, 36).

    PRAISE: Truth

    PRAYER: Our Father, reveal the truth to _____, and the truth shall make him/her free. I pray this in Jesus's name.

23. PROMISE: "And he is the propitiation for our sins: and not for ours only, but also for the sins of the whole world" (1 John 2:2 KJV).

    PRAISE: Savior

    PRAYER: Our Father, you forgave the adulteress taken in the very act, a sin punishable by death (John 8:1–12). Please, forgive _____ for his/her sins whatever they may be. I pray this in Jesus's name.

24. PROMISE: "And I, if I be lifted up from the earth, will draw all men unto me" (John 12:32 KJV).

    PRAISE: Mighty

PRAYER: Our Father, Jesus was lifted up from the earth in crucifixion, taking the punishment for our sins. Please, draw _____ back to Jesus (John 6:44). I pray this in Jesus's name.

25. PROMISE: "Draw nigh to God, and he will draw nigh to you" (James 4:8 KJV).

    PRAISE: Jehovah Shammah, The Lord Is There

    PRAYER: Our Father, I pray in Jesus's name that _____ will draw near to You.

26. PROMISE: "If any of you lacks wisdom, let him ask of God, who gives to all liberally and without reproach, and it will be given to him" (James 1:5).

    PRAISE: Wise

    PRAYER: Our Father, _____ needs wisdom that comes from You and not the world's wisdom. I pray in Jesus's name that he/she will ask for the wisdom that comes from You.

27. PROMISE: "For by grace you have been saved through faith, and that not of yourselves; it is the gift of God" (Ephesians 2:8).

    PRAISE: Adonai, Lord and Master

    PRAYER: Our Father, give _____ faith so he/she can please You. Help him/her to come to You, believing that You are, and that You are "a rewarder of them that diligently seek" You (Hebrews 11:6 KJV). I pray this in Jesus's name.

28. PROMISE: "Cast your bread upon the waters, For you will find it after many days" (Ecclesiastes 11:1).

PRAISE: Faithful

PRAYER: Our Father, I have prayed many prayers for _____ 's salvation, and I believe I will see it. His/her iniquity has caused him/her to stumble. I pray _____ will return to You, asking You to "Take away all iniquity" and to graciously receive him/her (Hosea 14:1–2 KJV).

29. PROMISE: "Who through faith subdued kingdoms, wrought righteousness, obtained promises, stopped the mouths of lions. Quenched the violence of fire, escaped the edge of the sword, out of weakness were made strong, waxed valiant in fight, turned to flight the armies of the aliens. Women received their dead raised to life again" (Hebrews 11:33–35 KJV).

PRAISE: Omnipotent, all-powerful God

PRAYER: Our Father, I am grateful for all of Your answers to my prayers and the work You have done in me and through me. I pray You will give me the faith and ability to subdue kingdoms, work righteousness, obtain promises, stop the lies of the devil, be made strong, become valiant in battle, and turn to flight the armies of Satan. In Jesus's name I pray.

PRAY–ER ENCOURAGEMENT: Like the woman healed because she pressed through the crowd until she reached Jesus, *press*! Press through whatever hinders you from praying. Press through whatever challenges your faith until you receive healing and victory from the Father for your prodigal. Press until you receive your promise from God. Remember the Father wants him or her to be saved more than you do, and He has the power to set your prodigal up for salvation. Keep pressing!

MARCH

OPEN

God got my attention.

When God brings a thought across my desk more than once, I become more aware. But August 16, 2018, God brought a concept into my life four times within an hour or so. Four times! My mind was on high alert! Many circumstances miraculously fell into place for me to receive this message so strongly from God from four very different avenues within that short span of time, which highlighted the importance of it even more.

The message was a prayer: *Open their eyes so they can see You; open their ears so they can hear You; open their minds so they can know You; open their hearts so they can receive You.*

Obviously, this prayer pertains to prodigals. The Bible tell us: "whose minds the god of this age has blinded, who do not believe, lest the light of the gospel of the glory of Christ, who is the image of God, should shine on them" (2 Corinthians 4:4). Satan has blinded them so they cannot see the truth! Now, doesn't that explain so much?

The good news comes a few verses later: "For it is the God who commanded light to shine out of darkness, who has shone in our hearts to give the light of the knowledge of the glory of God in the face of Jesus Christ" (v. 6). Of course, God is able to open their eyes to see Him! Of course, God is able to open their ears to hear Him! Of course, God is able to open their minds to know Him! Of course, God is able to open their hearts to receive whatever He has for them!

Soon the prayer evolved into one for myself and others for whom I pray. "'For My thoughts are not your thoughts, Nor are your ways My ways,' says the LORD. 'For as the heavens are higher than the earth, So are My ways higher than your ways, And My thoughts than your thoughts'" (Isaiah 55:8–9). Knowing this Scripture opens this concept to praying for ourselves so we can better know who God is and what He will and will not do, and so our desires mirror His will not only for our lives but for the prodigals for whom we pray, helping us to pray more in line with the will of God.

Months later this concept still comes at me from so many sources. God is not finished with this, so I am sharing it with you.

The Bible says, "No one can come to Me unless the Father who sent Me draws him; and I will raise him up at the last day" (John 6:44). God is calling us to ask Him to draw them and to open their eyes, ears, minds, and hearts.

1. PROMISE: "For it is the God who commanded light to shine out of darkness, who has shown in our hearts to give the light of the knowledge of the glory of God in the face of Jesus Christ" (2 Corinthians 4:6).

   PRAISE: Light

   PRAYER: Our Father, the god of this world has blinded _____ so he/she cannot see the light of the gospel. You are the God who commanded light to shine out of darkness. Please, shine Your light in _____'s heart so he/she will have knowledge of Your glory and see You again. I pray this in Jesus's name.

2. PROMISE: "Then the eyes of the blind shall be opened, and the ears of the deaf shall be unstopped" (Isaiah 35:5 KJV).

   PRAISE: Truth

PRAYER: Our Father, just as You opened the eyes of Elisha's servant to see the mountain full of horses and chariots, open _____'s eyes to see the truth of who You are, the One who can and will rescue him/her from sin (2 Kings 6:17). I pray this in Jesus's name.

3. PROMISE: "So Jesus had compassion on them, and touched their eyes: and immediately their eyes received sight, and they followed him" (Matthew 20:34 KJV).

   PRAISE: Compassionate

   PRAYER: Our Father, You asked two blind men what they wanted You to do for them, and they asked You to open their blinded eyes. That is what I am asking on _____'s behalf, that You open his/her eyes to truth. I pray this in Jesus's name.

4. PROMISE AND PRAISE: "Blessed be the LORD God, the God of Israel, Who only does wondrous things!" (Psalm 72:18).

   PRAYER: Our Father, open _____'s eyes so he/she may behold wondrous things from Your law (Psalm 119:18). In Jesus's name I pray.

5. PROMISE: "To open the blind eyes, to bring out the prisoners from the prison, and them that sit in darkness out of the prison house" (Isaiah 42:7 KJV).

   PRAISE: Omnipotent, all-powerful God

   PRAYER: Our Father, I pray _____'s eyes will be opened so he/she will be turned to light from darkness and to God instead of being controlled by Satan's power so his/her sins can be forgiven and he/she can be sanctified by faith in You (Acts 26:18). I pray this in Jesus's name.

6. PROMISE: "Then, looking up to heaven, He sighed, and said to him, 'Ephphatha,' that is, 'Be opened.' Immediately his ears were opened, and the impediment of his tongue was loosed, and he spoke plainly" (Mark 7:34–35).

   PRAISE: Jehovah Rapha, The Lord Our Healer

   PRAYER: Our Father, You are no respecter of persons (Acts 10:34). I ask that You will call out, "Ephphatha; be opened" to _____ and that his/her ears will be opened to Your truth. I pray this in Jesus's name.

7. PROMISE: "For the LORD gives wisdom; From His mouth come knowledge and understanding" (Proverbs 2:6).

   PRAISE: Wise—"Now unto the King eternal, immortal, invisible, the only wise God be honour and glory for ever and ever. Amen" (1 Timothy 1:17 KJV).

   PRAYER: Our Father, _____ is making bad decisions. Incline _____'s ear to wisdom and cause him/her to apply his/her heart to understanding. Move _____ to pray for discernment and understanding so he/she can understand the fear of You and find the knowledge of You (Proverbs 2:2–3, 5). I pray this in Jesus's name.

8. PROMISE: "A new heart also will I give you, and a new spirit will I put within you: and I will take away the stony heart out of your flesh, and I will give you an heart of flesh" (Ezekiel 36:26 KJV).

PRAISE: Elohim, Triune God, Creator

PRAYER: Our Father, take away the stony heart out of _____ 's flesh, and give him/her a heart of flesh. Put Your Spirit within him/her, and cause _____ to walk in Your statutes, keep Your judgments, and do them. I pray this in Jesus's name.

9. PROMISE: "I am sought of them that asked not for me; I am found of them that sought me not" (Isaiah 65:1 KJV).

    PRAISE: Life

    PRAYER: Our Father, I pray in Jesus's name against the darkened understanding, the alienation from the life of God, the ignorance, the blindness of heart, and the lack of feeling in _____ (Ephesians 4:18–19).

10. PROMISE: "And those who heard it said, 'Who then can be saved?' But He said, 'The things which are impossible with men are possible with God'" (Luke 18:26–27).

    PRAISE: Veil-Ripper

    PRAYER: Our Father, the gospel has been veiled to _____, and his/her mind has been blinded to keep him/her from believing (2 Corinthians 4:3). I pray that You will lift the veil in Jesus's name.

11. PROMISE: "Heaven and earth shall pass away, but my words shall not pass away" (Matthew 24:35 KJV).

    PRAISE: Immutable, never-changing

PRAYER: Our Father, I pray that the seed, the Word, will fall on good ground in _____'s heart, that his/her heart and mind will be prepared to receive that seed which has been and will be planted, and that it will take root and bring forth fruit thirty, sixty, a hundred fold (Matthew 13:8). I pray this in Jesus's name.

12. PROMISE: "And Jesus said, For judgment I am come into this world, that they which see not might see" (John 9:39 KJV).

PRAISE: Almighty God

PRAYER: Jesus, You came so _____ could see. Father, I ask that his/her eyes will no longer be closed to who You are, that he/she will see You. I pray this in Jesus's name.

13. PROMISE: "I have confidence in you, in the Lord, that you will have no other mind; but he who troubles you shall bear his judgment, whoever he is" (Galatians 5:10).

PRAISE: Deliverer

PRAYER: Our Father, _____ did run well, but someone hindered him/her so that he/she should not obey the truth (Galatians 5:7). I believe he/she will again believe nothing but truth. Cause him/her to let nothing hinder his/her salvation and walk with You. I pray this in Jesus's name.

14. PROMISE: "And I will bring the blind by a way that they knew not; I will lead them in paths that they have not known: I will make darkness light before them, and crooked things straight. These things will I do unto them, and not forsake them" (Isaiah 42:16 KJV).

PRAISE: Jehovah Raah, The Lord Our Shepherd

PRAYER: Our Father, I pray You will bring _____ by a way he/she does not know, lead him/her in paths he/she has not known. Make darkness light before him, and crooked things straight. Your word promises You will do these things and not forsake him/her. Give _____ hope in You. In Jesus's name I pray.

15. PROMISE: "I will put my law in their inward parts, and write it in their hearts; and will be their God, and they shall be my people" (Jeremiah 31:33 KJV).

PRAISE: Word

PRAYER: Our Father, put Your law in _____'s mind, and write it on his/her heart. Be his/her God. I pray this in Jesus's name.

16. PROMISE: "The LORD opens the eyes of the blind; The LORD raises those who are bowed down; The LORD loves the righteous" (Psalm 146:8).

PRAISE: Omniscient, all-knowing

PRAYER: Our Father, knowing all things about all people, three times You chose to use spit in the process of healing someone: the man who was deaf and had a speech impediment, and two blind men (Mark 7:32–35; Mark 8:22–25; John 9:1–7). You know what it will take to reach _____ and to open his/her spiritual eyes. I pray in Jesus's name that in Your omniscience, You will open his/her eyes to the truth.

17. PROMISE: "Who was before a blasphemer, and a persecutor, and injurious: but I obtained mercy, because I did it ignorantly in unbelief. And the grace of our Lord was exceeding abundant with faith and love which is in Christ Jesus. This is a faithful saying, and worthy of all acceptation, that Christ Jesus came into the world to save sinners; of whom I am chief" (1 Timothy 1:13–15 KJV).

PRAISE: Savior

PRAYER: Our Father, _____ seems far away from You like Paul was. I ask that he/she will see with his/her eyes, hear with his/her ears, and understand with his/her heart so that he/she can return, be healed, and be saved (Isaiah 6:10). In Jesus's name I pray.

18. PROMISE: "Listen to Me, you stubborn-hearted, Who are far from righteousness: I bring My righteousness near, it shall not be far off; My salvation shall not linger" (Isaiah 46:12–13).

PRAISE: Jehovah, Self-Existent One, I AM

PRAYER: Our Father, _____ says he/she does not believe in You. I ask You to open the grave which has him/her bound and bring him/her up out of that grave so he/she will know that You are the LORD (Ezekiel 37:13). I pray in Jesus's name.

19. PROMISE: "The hearing ear and the seeing eye, the LORD has made them both" (Proverbs 20:12).

PRAISE: Omnipotent, all-powerful

PRAYER: Our Father, bless _____'s eyes so he/she can see You and his/her ears so he/she can hear You (Matthew 13:16). I pray that he/she will seek Your face in Jesus's name.

20. PROMISE: "He uncovers deep things out of darkness, And brings the shadow of death to light" (Job 12:22).

    PRAISE: Light

    PRAYER: Our Father, enlighten _____'s eyes of understanding so he/she will know the hope that comes with being called by Christ and Your exceedingly great power toward believers (Ephesians 1:18–19). I pray this in Jesus's name.

21. PROMISE: "But Jesus answered them, 'My Father has been working until now, and I have been working'" (John 5:17).

    PRAISE: Word

    PRAYER: Our Father, I thank You for Your word. It brings me comfort in this fight for my prodigal. Cause _____ to give ear to Your law and to listen to the words of Your mouth (Psalm 78:1). Do not let him/her perish in his/her affliction (Psalm 119:92). I pray this in Jesus's name.

22. PROMISE: "So shall My word be that goes forth from My mouth; It shall not return to Me void, But it shall accomplish what I please, And it shall prosper in the thing for which I sent it" (Isaiah 55:11).

    PRAISE: Sovereign

PRAYER: Our Father, Your word promises that it will accomplish what You send it to do. Do not let anyone deceive _____ with persuasive words (Colossians 2:4). I pray that the devil will not be allowed to take the Word out of _____'s heart so that he/she can believe and be saved (Luke 8:12). I ask these things in Jesus's name.

23. PROMISE: "Nevertheless I tell you the truth; It is expedient for you that I go away: for if I go not away, the Comforter will not come unto you; but if I depart, I will send him unto you" (John 16:7 KJV).

PRAISE: Elohim, Triune God, Creator

PRAYER: Our Father, Your word says that "no man can say that Jesus is the Lord, but by the Holy Ghost" (1 Corinthians 12:3 KJV). I ask You to open _____'s mind to truth and grant that he/she can say Jesus is Lord. In Jesus's name I pray.

24. PROMISE: "And God said, Let there be light: and there was light" (Genesis 1:3 KJV).

PRAISE: Light

PRAYER: Our Father, cause _____ to no longer walk in the futility of his/her mind and no longer have his/her understanding darkened (Ephesians 4:17–18). I pray this in Jesus's name.

25. PROMISE: "Therefore He says: 'Awake, you who sleep, Arise from the dead, And Christ will give you light'" (Ephesians 5:14).

PRAISE: Worthy; El, God Most High

PRAYER: Our Father, eventually King Nebuchadnezzar came to his senses and praised You. I pray that _____ will also lift his/her eyes to heaven, and that You will return higher understanding to him/her. I pray he/she will bless You, the Most High, and praise and honor You Who lives forever (Daniel 4:34). In Jesus's name I pray.

26. PROMISE: "And they were not able to resist the wisdom and the Spirit by which he spoke" (Acts 6:10).

    PRAISE: Omniscient, all-knowing; wise

    PRAYER: Our Father, I pray You will send someone to _____ to speak to him/her with wisdom and the Spirit. Don't let _____ be wise in his/her own eyes; rather, cause him/her to fear You and depart from evil. You have promised this will be health to his/her flesh and strength to his/her bones (Proverbs 3:7–8). I pray this in Jesus's name.

27. PROMISE: "who desires all men to be saved and to come to the knowledge of the truth" (1 Timothy 2:4).

    PRAISE: Savior

    PRAYER: Our Father, I pray _____ will long to see Your face and "hear your voice; For your voice is sweet, And your face is lovely" (Song of Solomon 2:14). I ask that he/she will be saved and come to the knowledge of the truth. I pray these things in Jesus's name.

28. PROMISE: "'I will feed My flock, and I will make them lie down,' says the LORD GOD. 'I will seek what was lost and bring

back what was driven away, bind up the broken and strengthen what was sick'" (Ezekiel 34:15–16).

PRAISE: Adonai, Lord and Master

PRAYER: Our Father, I pray _____'s heart will know You. Cause him/her to come back to You wholeheartedly and make You his/her God (Jeremiah 24:7). I pray this in Jesus's name.

29. PROMISE: "Your ears shall hear a word behind you, saying, 'This is the way, walk in it,' Whenever you turn to the right hand Or whenever you turn to the left" (Isaiah 30:21).

PRAISE: Jehovah Raah, The Lord Our Shepherd

PRAYER: Our Father, whenever _____ turns to the right or left, open his/her ears and cause him/her to hear You speaking, telling him/her which way he/she should walk. Cause him/her to follow Your direction. I pray this in Jesus's name.

30. PROMISE: "God, who gives life to the dead and calls those things which do not exist as though they did" (Romans 4:17).

PRAISE: El Elyon, God Most High

PRAYER: Our Father, _____ is in rebellion against Your word. Help him/her to cry out to You and save him/her out of distress. Bring him/her out of darkness and the shadow of death and break his/her chains in pieces. Break "the gates of brass, and cut the bars of iron in sunder" (Psalm 107:11, 13-14, 16 KJV). I pray this in Jesus's name.

31. PROMISE: "But when Jesus perceived their thoughts, He answered and said to them, 'Why are you reasoning in your hearts?'" (Luke 5:22). Jesus knows _____'s very thoughts and can reach into his/her mind to show Himself, just like He did the scribes and Pharisees when He forgave the sins of the paralytic before healing him, showing He is the Son of God.

PRAISE: Omniscient, all-knowing

PRAYER: Prayer: Our Father, I pray _____ will no longer be "conformed to this world: but be ... transformed by the renewing of [his/her] mind" (Romans 12:2 KJV). I pray this in Jesus's name.

PRAY–ER ENCOURAGEMENT: As we pray these God-originated prayers at our church, awesomeness is happening. Raindrops are coming in from so many people, telling us that God is hearing and answering our prayers. He will do the same for you. (See April's introduction for explanation of the use of the term *raindrops*.) Let's pray against the hiding of truth so our prodigals can receive salvation and all the goodness God has for them in this world and for eternity. Let's touch God for our prodigals' salvation!

APRIL

RAINDROPS

Sometimes God's promises to us seem delayed, or maybe even like they are never going to happen. But God is always up to something!

There is a debate regarding whether or not it had ever rained on Earth before the flood during Noah's time. During creation, God had set up a different system of watering the earth, and it is suggested in the Bible that Noah had not seen a rainbow until after the flood waters had receded and he and his family were safely on land (Genesis 2:5-6, 8:15-16, 9:13). However, the Bible doesn't say, "Noah, it has never rained on the earth, and you do not even know what rain is, but water droplets are going to fall from the sky, and water will break up from underground, and there will be a flood. Water will cover the earth, so build an ark according to these specific plans, and you and your family will be saved."

Whether or not Noah witnessed any raindrops during the many years of building and stocking the ark, he diligently prepared a place of safety for his family because he took God at His word that a flood was eminent. We also must continue to work to protect our family spiritually through prayer even if not one raindrop of evidence comes to show that the promises are coming true. We pray until we see the deluge of answered prayers resulting in the salvation of our prodigals.

So many times, though, God gives us hints, little or big. I have a habit of using the term *raindrop* to identify these evidences of God's hand in the life of prodigals, proof that God is answering prayer, that His promises are true, and that we can take Him at His word. Throughout praying for your prodigal, watch for raindrops.

A raindrop can be

- A change in the life of your prodigal.
- Something your prodigal said or did which points to a change in ideas or actions.
- A theme God reveals to you through several sources.
- A Scripture God points out to you.
- A promise He speaks into your spirit.
- Someone revealing to you that God has given him or her a burden to pray for your prodigal.
- An ungodly influence removed from your prodigal's life.
- A new job or a promotion preventing partying all night.
- Your prodigal spending more time with family.
- So many other things.

Whatever is evidence that God hears your pleas and is answering becomes evidence of the rain, the deluge that is coming in your prodigal's life. Our God is creative, so very creative, and the raindrops can take any form He chooses. Watch for them. Write them down with dates (a place is provided in the last few pages of this book) and read them when you feel like no progress has been made. It will soon be evident to you that God indeed has heard and is answering you. Give Him thanks for His active hand working in the life of your prodigal.

And then pray and watch for the deluge!

1. PROMISE AND PRAISE: "Who is like You, O LORD, among the gods? Who is like You, glorious in holiness, Fearful in praises, doing wonders?" (Exodus 15:11).

   PRAYER: Our Father, bring _____ up out the horrible pit and miry clay that he/she is in. Set his/her feet on a rock and establish his/her steps. Put a new song in _____'s mouth (Psalm 40:2–3). I pray this in Jesus's name.

2. PROMISE: "O Lᴏʀᴅ Gᴏᴅ, You have begun to show Your servant Your greatness and Your mighty hand, for what god is there in heaven or on earth who can do anything like Your works and Your mighty deeds?" (Deuteronomy 3:24).

    PRAISE: El Shaddai, Almighty, All-Sufficient God—"And He said to me, 'My grace is sufficient for you, for My strength is made perfect in weakness'" (2 Corinthians 12:9).

    PRAYER: Our Father, I pray _____ will work out his/her "own salvation with fear and trembling" (Philippians 2:12 KJV). In Jesus's name I pray.

3. PROMISE: "Then the fire of the Lᴏʀᴅ fell, and consumed the burnt sacrifice, and the wood, and the stones, and the dust, and licked up the water that was in the trench. And when all the people saw it, they fell on their faces: and they said, The Lᴏʀᴅ he is the God; the Lᴏʀᴅ, he is the God" (1 Kings 18:38–39 KJV).

    PRAISE: God is able!

    PRAYER: Our Father, You consumed Elijah's sacrifice through a miracle. I ask You to work a miracle in _____'s life. Light him/her on fire for You. Like You showed Yourself to the lost children of Israel, convincing them You alone are God, causing them to turn to You, show Yourself strong in _____'s life and cause him/her to turn to You. I pray this in Jesus's name.

4. PROMISE: "You have turned for me my mourning into dancing; You have put off my sackcloth and clothed me with gladness, To the end that my glory may sing praise to You and not be silent. O Lᴏʀᴅ my God, I will give thanks to You forever" (Psalm 30:11–12).

PRAISE: Worthy—"You are worthy, O Lord, To receive glory and honor and power; For You created all things, And by Your will they exist and were created" (Revelation 4:11).

PRAYER: Our Father, I pray _____ will enter Your presence with thanksgiving and praise, be thankful to You, and bless Your name (Psalm 100:4). I pray this in Jesus's name.

5. PROMISE: "Come and see the works of God; He is awesome in His doing toward the sons of men" (Psalm 66:5).

   PRAISE: El Shaddai, Almighty, All-Sufficient God

   PRAYER: Our Father, I pray in Jesus's name that _____ will have faith and hope, believing in the things not seen (Hebrews 11:1).

6. PROMISE: "For You are great, and do wondrous things; You alone are God" (Psalm 86:10).

   PRAISE: Omniscient, all-knowing

   PRAYER: Our Father, give _____ "wisdom that is from above" and "is first pure, then peaceable, gentle, and easy to be intreated, full of mercy and good fruits, without partiality, and without hypocrisy" (James 3:17 KJV). In Jesus's name I pray.

7. PROMISE AND PRAISE: "Oh, sing to the LORD a new song! For He has done marvelous things; His right hand and His holy arm have gained Him the victory" (Psalm 98:1).

   PRAYER: Our Father, I pray _____ will not "give place to the devil" (Ephesians 4:27) but will present his/her body "a living sacrifice, holy, acceptable to" You (Romans 12:1). I pray this in Jesus's name.

8. PROMISE: "God is the LORD, And He has given us light" (Psalm 118:27).

    PRAISE: Light

    PRAYER: Our Father, You are the LORD, and Your Word says You have given us light. You have. Let _____ see Your light and know the truth. I pray this in Jesus's name.

9. PROMISE: "The LORD has done great things for us, And we are glad" (Psalm 126:3).

    PRAISE: Savior

    PRAYER: Our Father, do not look at _____'s sins, and erase all his/her iniquities (Psalm 51:9). I pray this in Jesus's name.

10. PROMISE: "Sing to the LORD, For He has done excellent things; This is known in all the earth" (Isaiah 12:5).

    PRAISE: El Elyon, God Most High

    PRAYER: Our Father, we taught _____ about You from his/her youth. I pray he/she will remember, believe, and declare Your wondrous works (Psalm 71:17). I pray this in Jesus's name.

11. PROMISE: "So I prophesied as he commanded me, and the breath came into them, and they lived, and stood up upon their feet, an exceeding great army" (Ezekiel 37:10 KJV).

    PRAISE: Life

    PRAYER: Our Father, like You raised up the dry bones through Ezekiel, raise up _____ and other prodigals into an "exceeding great army" for Your kingdom. Use us and our prayers as You see fit to accomplish this. I pray this in Jesus's name.

12. PROMISE: "Call to Me, and I will answer you, and show you great and mighty things, which you do not know" (Jeremiah 33:3). If you are not seeing raindrops with your prodigal, ask God to show you.

    PRAISE: Merciful

    PRAYER: Our Father, restore _____ and look at him/her with approval so he/she will be saved (Psalm 80:3). I pray this in Jesus's name.

13. PROMISE: Speaking of sons, the LORD says, "Lift up your eyes, look around and see; All these gather together and come to you" (Isaiah 49:18).

    PRAISE: Redeemer

    PRAYER: Our Father, cause Your kingdom to come to our family, to _____, and gather our prodigals back (Matthew 6:10). I pray this in Jesus's name.

14. PROMISE: "And the light shines in the darkness, and the darkness did not comprehend it" (John 1:5).

    PRAISE: Light

    PRAYER: Our Father, enlighten _____'s darkness. I pray this in Jesus's name.

15. PROMISE: "And we know that all things work together for good to them that love God, to them who are the called according to his purpose" (Romans 8:28 KJV).

    PRAISE: Sovereign

    PRAYER: Our Father, I ask in Jesus's name that Your will be done in _____'s life just as Your will is done in heaven (Matthew 6:10).

16. PROMISE: "God has dealt to each one a measure of faith" (Romans 12:3).

    PRAISE: Adonai, Lord and Master

    PRAYER: Our Father, thank You for the measure of faith You have given _____. Let that faith take root in him/her and grow into salvation. I pray this in Jesus's name.

17. PROMISE: "Blessed be the God and Father of our Lord Jesus Christ, who has blessed us with every spiritual blessing in the heavenly places in Christ, just as He chose us in Him before the foundation of the world, that we should be holy and without blame before Him in love" (Ephesians 1:3–4).

PRAISE: Holy

PRAYER: Our Father, thank You for every spiritual blessing and for choosing to give Your Son to all. I pray in Jesus's name that _____ will be presented "holy, and blameless, and above reproach" in Your sight (Colossians 1:22).

18. PROMISE: "The darkness is passing away, and the true light is already shining" (1 John 2:8).

    PRAISE: Light

    PRAYER: Our Father, circumcise the heart of my descendants, of _____ specifically, to love You with all his/her heart and soul, so that he/she may live (Deuteronomy 30:6). I pray this in Jesus's name.

19. PROMISE: "The voice of rejoicing and salvation Is in the tents of the righteous; The right hand of the LORD does valiantly" (Psalm 118:15).

    PRAISE: Omnipotent, all-powerful

    PRAYER: Our Father, open the gates of righteousness to _____, and cause him/her to go through them so that he/she will praise You. I ask this in Jesus's name.

20. PROMISE: "Unto the upright there arises light in the darkness; He is gracious, and full of compassion, and righteous" (Psalm 112:4).

    PRAISE: Light—"That was the true Light which gives light to *every* man coming into the world" (John 1:9, emphasis mine).

PRAYER: Our Father, I pray in Jesus's name that _____ will "have no fellowship with the unfruitful works of darkness, but rather reprove them" (Ephesians 5:11 KJV).

21. PROMISE: "But if we walk in the light as He is in the light, we have fellowship with one another, and the blood of Jesus Christ His Son cleanses us from all sin" (1 John 1:7). Notice the word *all*.

    PRAISE: Light

    PRAYER: Our Father, thank You for all You have already done to bring _____ back to You. Cause him/her to walk in the light and cleanse him/her from all sin. I pray this in Jesus's name.

22. PROMISE: "When the LORD brought back the captivity of Zion, We were like those who dream. Then our mouth was filled with laughter, And our tongue with singing. Then they said among the nations, 'The LORD has done great things for them'" (Psalm 126:1–2).

    PRAISE: Redeemer

    PRAYER: Our Father, I pray _____ will be brought back from captivity as You did Zion. You have already done great things for him/her, and I pray he/she will remember them and shout joyfully before You, gladly serve You, and come before Your presence with singing (Psalm 100:1-2 KJV). I pray this in Jesus's name.

23. PROMISE: Speaking of seed, Jesus said, "And other fell on good ground, and did yield fruit that sprang up and increased; and

brought forth, some thirty, and some sixty, and some an hundred" (Mark 4:8 KJV).

PRAISE: Word

PRAYER: Our Father, cause _____ to receive Your words and treasure Your commands within himself/herself (Proverbs 2:1). I pray this in Jesus's name.

24. PROMISE: "Then He said, 'To what shall we liken the kingdom of God? Or with what parable shall we picture it? It is like a mustard seed which, when it is sown on the ground, is smaller than all the seeds on earth; but when it is sown, it grows up and becomes greater than all herbs, and shoots out large branches, so that the birds of the air may nest under its shade'" (Mark 4:30–32).

PRAISE: Life

PRAYER: Our Father, I pray the kingdom of God will be sown in _____'s life and will grow up and become mighty, bringing him/her to fulfill the purpose You have for him/her. In Jesus's name I pray.

25. PROMISE: "Now I rejoice, not that you were made sorry, but that your sorrow led to repentance. For you were made sorry in a godly manner, that you might suffer loss from us in nothing. For godly sorrow produces repentance leading to salvation, not to be regretted; but the sorrow of the world produces death" (2 Corinthians 7:9–10).

PRAISE: Compassionate

PRAYER: Our Father, give _____ a godly sorrow that will lead to repentance, a repentance that will lead to salvation. I pray this in Jesus's name.

26. PROMISE: "He delivers and rescues, And He works signs and wonders In heaven and on earth" (Daniel 6:27).

PRAISE: El Elyon, God Most High

PRAYER: Our Father, I pray _____ will exalt You for Your greatness, power, glory, victory, and majesty, and as head over the kingdom and all that is in the earth and heaven (1 Chronicles 29:11). In Jesus's name I pray.

27. PROMISE: "O LORD, for Your servant's sake, and according to Your own heart, You have done all this greatness, in making known all these great things. O LORD, there is none like You, nor is there any God besides You, according to all that we have heard with our ears" (1 Chronicles 17:19–20).

PRAISE: El Elyon, God Most High

PRAYER: Our Father, please, let _____ know there is no wisdom or understanding or counsel that is against the LORD (Proverbs 21:30). In Jesus's name I pray.

28. PROMISE: "Through the LORD's mercies we are not consumed, Because His compassions fail not. They are new every morning; Great is Your faithfulness" (Lamentations 3:22–23).

PRAISE: Merciful

PRAYER: Our Father, revive _____ according to Your lovingkindness (Psalm 119:88). I pray this in Jesus's name.

29. PROMISE: "For it is God who works in you both to will and to do for His good pleasure" (Philippians 2:13).

PRAISE: Sovereign

PRAYER: Our Father, I pray in Jesus's name that _____ will stand perfect and complete in Your will (Colossians 4:12).

30. PROMISE: "being confident of this very thing, that He who has begun a good work in you will complete it until the day of Jesus Christ" (Philippians 1:6).

PRAISE: El-Shaddai, Almighty, All-Sufficient God

PRAYER: Our Father, I am confident of this very thing, that You have begun a good work in _____ in answer to my prayers, and I thank You for working when I can see and when I cannot. I ask in Jesus's name that You will complete that work until the day of Christ.

PRAY-ER ENCOURAGEMENT: You may have heard it said that April showers bring May flowers. I do believe the prayers we have prayed this month will bring answers from God. After all, He promised: "And whatever things you ask in prayer, believing, you will receive" (Matthew 21:22). Even if you are not *seeing* raindrops in answers to your prayers, still know that God is working to bring your prodigal back to Himself.

Tami Winkelman

MAY

CATCHING UP

One weekend I asked our Life Church Huntsville Prayer for Prodigals team to come prepared to share their favorite biblical promise. Each promise shared was as individual as they are. Most likely your favorite promise speaks to you because of your situation with your prodigal. The Bible is wonderful in that way, speaking to us in the different circumstances of life, giving hope, real hope, where we need it most.

When God makes a promise, it is different from when we make a promise. My husband knows that if I say I will do something, it is my full intention to do so, but there are times something prohibits my carrying out my full intention: traffic, sickness, an unexpected interruption, long lines at the store, or I may simply forget.

But when God makes a promise, *He always keeps it!* He never forgets, and He is always capable.

There are two reasons God can make a promise: because of who He is, and because of what He knows.

WHO HE IS:

- Omnipresent, present in all times as well as places—Speaking of God's omnipresence in time, Isaiah 57:15 tells us that He inhabits eternity: "For thus says the High and Lofty One Who inhabits eternity, whose name is Holy." Psalm 90:2 says it another way: "Before the mountains were brought forth, Or ever You had formed the earth and the world, Even from everlasting

56

to everlasting, You are God." He already exists in the future, into the everlasting.

- Sovereign—David describes it beautifully in 1 Chronicles 29:11–12:

> Yours, O LORD, is the greatness,
> The power and the glory,
> The victory and the majesty;
> For all that is in heaven and in earth is Yours;
> Yours is the kingdom, O LORD,
> And You are exalted as head over all.
> Both riches and honor come from You,
> And You reign over all.
> In Your hand is power and might;
> In Your hand it is to make great
> And to give strength to all.

- Omnipotent, all-powerful God—He simply can! (1 Chronicles 29:11 above).

WHAT HE KNOWS:

- Since He is already in eternity, He already sees what has happened! He is already seeing it! He is already seeing those prayers answered and that promise a reality!

Isn't that incredible?

Guess what our job is in this endeavor: to love our prodigals and prayerfully wait until we catch up! We wait until we get to the place in time when the promise is already reality, until we witness first-hand what God has *already done* in the lives of our prodigals!

Doesn't that make the wait a little easier?

1. PROMISE: "The LORD will fight for you, and you shall hold your peace" (Exodus 14:14).

   PRAISE: El Elyon, God Most High

PRAYER: Our Father, make _____ complete in You, "the head of all principality and power" (Colossians 2:10 KJV). In Jesus's name I pray.

2. PROMISE: "But from there you will seek the LORD your God, and you will find Him if you seek Him with all your heart and with all your soul" (Deuteronomy 4:29).

   PRAISE: Adonai, Lord and Master

   PRAYER: Our Father, I pray in Jesus's name that _____ will seek You with all his/her heart and soul and find You.

3. PROMISE: "When you are in distress, and all these things come upon you in the latter days, when you turn to the LORD your God and obey His voice (for the LORD your God is a merciful God), He will not forsake you nor destroy you, nor forget the covenant of your fathers which He swore to them" (Deuteronomy 4:30–31).

   PRAISE: Merciful

   PRAYER: Our Father, show _____ Your ways and teach him/her Your paths. Lead _____ in Your truth, and teach him/her; because You are the God of his/her salvation. Remember Your tender mercies and loving kindnesses (Psalm 25:4–6). I pray this in Jesus's name.

4. PROMISE: "And all these blessings shall come upon you and overtake you, because you obey the voice of the LORD your God. … Blessed shall be the fruit of your body" (Deuteronomy 28:2, 4).

PRAISE: Sovereign—"Yours, O LORD, is the greatness, The power and the glory, The victory and the majesty; For all that is in heaven and in earth is Yours; Yours is the kingdom, O LORD, And You are exalted as head over all" (1 Chronicles 29:11).

PRAYER: Our Father, we are obedient in praying for our children. Please, bless _____ with salvation. I pray this in Jesus's name.

5. PROMISE: "The LORD will cause your enemies who rise against you to be defeated before your face; they shall come out against you one way and flee before you seven ways" (Deuteronomy 28:7).

   PRAISE: Jehovah Nissi, The Lord Our Banner—He fights for His children against the enemy of the soul.

   PRAYER: Our Father, I pray in Jesus's name that You will defeat the enemies of _____'s soul. Cause them to flee seven ways.

6. PROMISE: "The LORD will open to you His good treasure, the heavens, to give the rain to your land in its season, and to bless all the work of your hand" (Deuteronomy 28:12).

   PRAISE: Father

   PRAYER: Our Father, we raised _____ to serve You. That is the work of our hands. Please, bless that work by opening the heavens over him/her and filling him/her with all the fullness of You. I pray this in Jesus's name.

7. PROMISE: "There is no one like the God of Jeshurun, Who rides the heavens to help you, And in His excellency on the clouds. The eternal God is your refuge, And underneath are the everlasting arms; He will thrust out the enemy from before you, And will say, 'Destroy!'" (Deuteronomy 33:26–27).

    PRAISE: Deliverer

    PRAYER: Our Father, cause _____ to trust in You and to say You are his/her God. His/her times are in Your control. Deliver my prodigal from his/her enemies' hands. I pray this in Jesus's name.

8. PROMISE: "And now, O Lord GOD, You are God, and Your words are true" (2 Samuel 7:28).

    PRAISE: Promise Keeper

    PRAYER: Jesus, you told the nobleman in Galilee that his son lived. God, cause my child to live, really live, in You. Like that father, I believe Your word (John 4:50). I pray this in Jesus's name.

9. PROMISE: "but my righteousness shall be for ever, and my salvation from generation to generation" (Isaiah 51:8 KJV).

    PRAISE: Savior

    PRAYER: "I long for Your salvation, O LORD," for _____ (Psalm 119:174). Please, save him/her because of Your great name. I pray this in Jesus's name.

10. PROMISE: "For You have armed me with strength for the battle; You have subdued under me those who rose against me" (2 Samuel 22:40).

PRAISE: Omnipotent, all-powerful God

PRAYER: Our Father, I pray _____ will put on Your whole armor so that he/she can withstand the devil's plans (Ephesians 6:11). I pray this in Jesus's name.

11. PROMISE: "LORD God of Israel, there is no God in heaven above or on earth below like You, who keep Your covenant and mercy with Your servants who walk before You with all their hearts" (1 Kings 8:23).

PRAISE: El Elyon, God Most High

PRAYER: Our Father, I endeavor to walk before You with all my heart, and I pray in Jesus's name that _____ will also follow You and no other gods.

12. PROMISE: "But I know your dwelling place, Your going out and your coming in, And your rage against Me" (Isaiah 37:28; 2 Kings 19:27).

PRAISE: Omniscient, all-knowing God

PRAYER: Our Father, You know _____'s dwelling place and his/her comings and goings, where he/she is at all times, and for that I am grateful. You also know the reasons he/she left serving You. Father, I pray You will set everything right in his/her life and rescue him/her from Satan's control. In Jesus's name I pray.

13. PROMISE: "As for you, my son Solomon, know the God of your father, and serve Him with a loyal heart and with a willing mind; for the LORD searches all hearts and understands all the intent of the thoughts. If you seek Him, He will be found by you" (1 Chronicles 28:9).

PRAISE: Adonai, Lord and Master

PRAYER: Our Father, I pray _____ will know You, my God, and serve You with a loyal heart and a willing mind. I pray he/she will seek You and find You. I ask these things in Jesus's name.

14. PROMISE: "And he said, 'Listen, all you of Judah and you inhabitants of Jerusalem, and you, King Jehoshaphat! Thus says the LORD to you: "Do not be afraid nor dismayed because of this great multitude, for the battle is not yours, but God's"'" (2 Chronicles 20:15).

PRAISE: El, God Of Power And Might

PRAYER: Our Father, draw _____ out of many waters. Deliver him/her from the strong enemy and those who hate him/her. The enemy is too strong for him/her but not for You (Psalm 18:16–17). Please, show Yourself mighty in _____'s life. I pray this in Jesus's name.

15. PROMISE: "Be strong and courageous, be not afraid nor dismayed for the king of Assyria, nor for all the multitude that is with him: for there be more with us than with him: with him is an arm of flesh; but with us is the LORD our God to help us, and to fight our battles" (2 Chronicles 32:7–8 KJV).

PRAISE: El Olam, Everlasting God

PRAYER: Our Father, bless _____ indeed and let Your hand be with him/her. Keep my prodigal from evil so that it will not hurt him/her. I pray this in Jesus's name.

16. PROMISE: "The righteous cry out, and the LORD hears, And delivers them out of all their troubles" (Psalm 34:17).

    PRAISE: Deliverer

    PRAYER: Our Father, I pray You will deliver _____ "from the way of evil, From the man who speaks perverse things" (Proverbs 2:12). I pray this in Jesus's name.

17. PROMISE: "When he slew them, then they sought him: and they returned and enquired early after God. And they remembered that God was their rock, and the high God their redeemer" (Psalm 78:34–35 KJV).

    PRAISE: Sovereign

    PRAYER: Our Father, the children of Israel turned back to You and sought You when they needed to be delivered. Cause _____ to turn at Your rebuke; pour out Your Spirit on him/her and make known Your words to him/her (Proverbs 1:23). I pray this in Jesus's name.

18. PROMISE: "The children of Your servants will continue, And their descendants will be established before You" (Psalm 102:28).

    PRAISE: Counselor

PRAYER: Our Father, please cause _____ to acknowledge You in all his/her ways and direct his/her paths not only for himself/herself, but for the good of his/her descendants (Proverbs 3:6). I pray this in Jesus's name.

19. PROMISE: "But the mercy of the LORD is from everlasting to everlasting upon them that fear him, and his righteousness unto children's children" (Psalm 103:17 KJV).

    PRAISE: Jehovah Tsidkenu, The Lord Our Righteousness

    PRAYER: Our Father, Your mercy and righteousness are available to _____. Cause him/her to walk in Your gift of mercy and righteousness and to know Your great love for him/her (John 15:13). I pray this in Jesus's name.

20. PROMISE: "Praise the LORD! Blessed is the man who fears the LORD, Who delights greatly in His commandments. His descendants will be mighty on earth; The generation of the upright will be blessed" (Psalm 112:1–2).

    PRAISE: Adonai, Lord and Master

    PRAYER: Our Father, I pray that _____ will be wise so that he/she will fear and depart from evil (Proverbs 14:16). In Jesus's name I pray.

21. PROMISE: "He will not allow your foot to be moved; He who keeps you will not slumber. Behold, He who keeps Israel Shall neither slumber nor sleep. The LORD is your keeper; The LORD is your shade at your right hand" (Psalm 121:3–5).

    PRAISE: Jehovah, Self-Existent One, Lord, Lord God

PRAYER: Our Father, the day and night are Yours (Psalm 74:16). Draw _____ during the day and during the night, while he/she is awake and even while he/she sleeps. I pray this in Jesus's name.

22. PROMISE: "Unto the upright there arises light in the darkness; He is gracious, and full of compassion, and righteous" (Psalm 112:4).

PRAISE: Light

PRAYER: Our Father, send out Your light and Your truth to _____. Let Your light and truth lead him/her. I pray this in Jesus's name.

23. PROMISE: "And he will destroy in this mountain the face of the covering cast over all people, and the vail that is spread over all nations" (Isaiah 25:7 KJV).

PRAISE: Veil-Lifter

PRAYER: Our Father, cause _____ to turn to You, and take the veil away (2 Corinthians 3:16). I pray this in Jesus's name.

24. PROMISE: "I will be found by you, says the LORD, and I will bring you back from your captivity" (Jeremiah 29:14).

PRAISE: Deliverer

PRAYER: Our Father, _____ has been taken captive by Satan. He/she is so bound. I pray that my prodigal will find You, and that You will bring him/her back from his/her captivity.

25. PROMISE AND PRAISE: "Blessed are You, LORD God of Israel, our Father, forever and ever. Yours, O LORD, is the greatness, The power and the glory, The victory and the majesty; For all that is in heaven and in earth is Yours; Yours is the kingdom, O LORD, And You are exalted as head over all. Both riches and honor come from You, And You reign over all. In Your hand is power and might; In Your hand it is to make great And to give strength to all. Now therefore, our God, We thank You And praise Your glorious name" (1 Chronicles 29:10–13).

PRAYER: Our Father, please bring health and healing to _____. Reveal Your abundant peace and truth to him/her (Jeremiah 33:6). I pray this in Jesus's name.

26. PROMISE: "Thus says the Lord GOD: 'Behold, I will lift My hand in an oath to the nations, And set up My standard for the peoples; They shall bring your sons in their arms, And your daughters shall be carried on their shoulders'" (Isaiah 49:22).

PRAISE: Jehovah Nissi, The Lord Our Banner—our banner, our flag, our ensign is the Lord.

PRAYER: Our Father, You understand _____'s path as well as his/her rest. You know all his/her ways (Psalm 139:3). Direct my prodigal's path straight back to You. Use every moment of his/her life, asleep and awake, to speak to him/her. I pray this in Jesus's name.

27. PROMISE: "You, who have shown me great and severe troubles, Shall revive me again, And bring me up again from the depths of the earth" (Psalm 71:20).

PRAISE: Sovereign

PRAYER: Our Father, I raised _____ to serve You and not Satan. I did not raise him/her for trouble (Isaiah 65:23a). I pray he/she will "Walk in the Spirit and … not fulfil the lust of the flesh" (Galatians 5:16 KJV). I ask in Jesus's name.

28. PROMISE: "And I will give them one heart, and I will put a new spirit within you; and I will take the stony heart out of their flesh, and will give them an heart of flesh: That they may walk in my statutes, and keep mine ordinances, and do them: and they shall be my people, and I will be their God" (Ezekiel 11:19–20 KJV).

    PRAISE: Jehovah M'Kaddesh, The Lord Who Sanctifies

    PRAYER: Our Father, put a new spirit in _____. Remove his/her stony heart and give him/her a soft and teachable heart. Cause him/her to walk according to Your commandments. Show him/her that he/she is Yours, and that You are his/her God. I pray this in Jesus's name.

29. PROMISE: "And I will give them one heart, and one way, that they may fear me for ever, for the good of them, and of their children after them" (Jeremiah 32:39 KJV).

    PRAISE: The Way

    PRAYER: Our Father, create in _____ a clean heart, O God; and "renew a right spirit" in him/her (Psalm 51:10 KJV). I pray this in Jesus's name.

30. PROMISE: "It may be that the house of Judah will hear all the adversities which I purpose to bring upon them, that everyone may turn from his evil way, that I may forgive their iniquity and their sin" (Jeremiah 36:3).

PRAISE: The way, truth, and life

PRAYER: Our Father, You have set life and death, blessing and cursing before me. Help me to choose life so that _____ and I may live. Also, help us to choose life and to love, obey, and cling to You, for You are life and length of days (Deuteronomy 30:19–20). I ask that _____ will take heed to the warnings in Your word. I pray these things in Jesus's name.

31. PROMISE: "And it shall come to pass afterward, that I will pour out my spirit upon all flesh; and your sons and your daughters shall prophesy, your old men shall dream dreams, your young men shall see visions" (Joel 2:28 KJV).

PRAISE: Worthy

PRAYER: Our Father, I pray _____ will remember You in the days of his/her youth (Ecclesiastes 12:1). Save _____ and pour out Your Spirit on him/her. I pray this in Jesus's name.

PRAY-ER ENCOURAGEMENT: We should be careful to claim only the promises which are meant for us or our prodigals and not take ideas out of context. We *know* it is God's perfect will for our prodigals to be saved (2 Peter 3:9). We *know* Jesus Himself is the Advocate with the Father for our prodigals (1 John 2:1). We also *know* God has a specific plan for good for our prodigals (Jeremiah 29:11; Romans 8:28). There are so many other promises, too, so let's claim those and pray accordingly, building our faith in God, taking Him at His word.

JUNE

GOD HAS THIS

Have you ever been so worried, so upset, or so sad about your prodigal you couldn't breathe?

Has the pain been so intense you didn't know if you could survive?

Have you ever felt destitute, like the situation would never change, no matter how hard you prayed?

Have you ever left like your prayers were ineffective, like God answers other people's prayers but apparently not yours?

Have you ever questioned the very existence of God because heaven seemed silent?

We can become so distraught over Satan's apparent victory in the lives of our prodigals that we are almost paralyzed. We become so overwhelmed all we can do is cry and pray and beg God to work, to change things, but sometimes things seem to get worse. Begging isn't the answer.

Little by little, God showed me the answer, something that helps me, and I want to share it with you. It is so simple but, yet, profound. I now *know* God is working to bring our prodigals back to Himself. I know because He promised to answer if we ask, and we have asked. I know because His word says so.

Yes, sometimes I am still blindsided, and a phone call can *seemingly* change everything, but three phrases come back to me that restores my faith.

- God has this.
- He is Faithful.

- I can trust Him.

God has this. It doesn't matter what *this* is; if you have committed it to God through prayer, He has it. "The LORD will fight for you, and you shall hold your peace" (Exodus 14:14). It may seem hopeless, but it isn't. God has this.

The Bible tells us: "Behold, the LORD'S hand is not shortened, that it cannot save; neither his ear heavy, that it cannot hear" (Isaiah 59:1 KJV). It does not matter how far into sin your prodigal is, God has your *this*! He can even change the heart and save those who say they don't believe in Him. I know of three people who once claimed to be atheists but now know and serve the Lord. Two of them are presently pastors. God can save anyone!

God has this situation with your prodigal, and His hand is not shortened. Continue to trust Him.

1. PROMISE: "Then Job answered the LORD and said: 'I know that You can do everything, and that no purpose of Yours can be withheld from You'" (Job 42:1–2).

   PRAISE: Sovereign

   PRAYER: Our Father, cause _____ to put on the Lord Jesus Christ and make no provision for the flesh, to fulfill its lusts (Romans 13:14). In Jesus's name I pray.

2. PROMISE: "The LORD brings the counsel of the nations to nothing; He makes the plans of the peoples of no effect" (Psalm 33:10).

   PRAISE: Counselor

   PRAYER: Our Father, cause _____ to not walk in the counsel of the ungodly, nor stand in sinners' paths, nor sit in the seat of the scornful. Let him/her delight in Your law, and cause him/her to meditate in it day and night (Psalm 1:1–2). I pray this in Jesus's name.

3. PROMISE: "Our God is the God of salvation; And to GOD the Lord belong escapes from death" (Psalm 68:20).

    PRAISE: Life

    PRAYER: Our Father God, _____ is dead in trespasses. Make him/her alive with Christ, and save him/her by Your grace (Ephesians 2:5). I pray this in Jesus's name.

4. PROMISE: "For God is my King of old, working salvation in the midst of the earth" (Psalm 74:12 KJV).

    PRAISE: Adonai, Lord and Master

    PRAYER: Our Father, I am so thankful You are working salvation throughout the earth. I pray in Jesus's name that _____ would long for Your salvation, and that Your law would be his/her delight (Psalm 119:174).

5. PROMISE: "You are the God who does wonders; You have declared Your strength among the peoples" (Psalm 77:14).

    PRAISE: Great—"For You are great, and do wondrous things; You alone are God" (Psalm 86:10).

    PRAYER: Our Father, I pray that when _____ is saved those around him/her will see the change, that the change will be a witness to them of You, and that his/her light will shine before men so that his/her good works will be evidence, bringing You glory (Matthew 5:16). I pray this in Jesus's name.

6. PROMISE: "You have a mighty arm; Strong is Your hand, and high is Your right hand" (Psalm 89:13).

   PRAISE: Mighty

   PRAYER: Our Father, lead _____ and hold him/her with Your right hand no matter where he/she goes (Psalm 139:7–10). I pray this in Jesus's name.

7. PROMISE: "Who forgives all your iniquities, Who heals all your diseases, Who redeems your life from destruction, Who crowns you with lovingkindness and tender mercies" (Psalm 103:3–4).

   PRAISE: Redeemer

   PRAYER: Our Father, _____ has chosen a path that is destroying him/her. I pray You will redeem his/her life from destruction, forgive him/her of all iniquities, and crown him/her with lovingkindness and tender mercies. I pray this in Jesus's name.

8. PROMISE: "The right hand of the LORD is exalted; the right hand of the LORD does valiantly" (Psalm 118:16).

   PRAISE: Omnipotent, all-powerful

   PRAYER: Our Father, _____ is in a yoke of bondage to Satan. When you free him/her, cause him/her to stay steady in that freedom and not to ever become "entangled again with the yoke of bondage" (Galatians 5:1 KJV). I pray this in Jesus's name.

9. PROMISE: "The LORD shall preserve you from all evil; He shall preserve your soul" (Psalm 121:7).

   PRAISE: Defense

   PRAYER: Our Father, I pray in Jesus's name that You preserve _____ from all evil and preserve his soul.

10. PROMISE: "The LORD shall preserve your going out and your coming in From this time forth, and even forevermore" (Psalm 121:8).

    PRAISE: Shield

    PRAYER: Our Father, I pray _____ will walk with wise people and be wise (Proverbs 13:20). I pray this in Jesus's name.

11. PROMISE: "O LORD, You have searched me and known me. You know my sitting down and my rising up; You understand my thought afar off" (Psalm 139:1–2).

    PRAISE: Omniscient, all-knowing

    PRAYER: Our Father, you have searched and known _____; You know when he/she sits and rises; You know his/her thought afar off. LORD, please, pursue my prodigal in ways that will reach him/her. Thank You for always being aware of him/her. I pray this in Jesus's name.

12. PROMISE: "You have hedged me behind and before, And laid Your hand upon me. Such knowledge is too wonderful for me; It is high, I cannot attain it" (Psalm 139:5–6).

PRAISE: Jehovah Sabaoth, Lord Of Hosts, Commander of the armies of heaven

PRAYER: Our Father, I ask that You hedge _____ in, behind and before, and lay Your hand upon him/her. Fortify this hedge with your angels as guards. Keep _____ from evil and keep evil from him/her. I pray this in Jesus's name.

13. PROMISE: "If I take the wings of the morning, And dwell in the uttermost parts of the sea, Even there Your hand shall lead me, And Your right hand shall hold me" (Psalm 139:9–10).

    PRAISE: Jehovah Shammah, The Lord Is There

    PRAYER: Our Father, I pray that _____ will choose his/her friends carefully so the way of the wicked will not lead him/her astray (Proverbs 12:26). Cause my prodigal to let no man deceive him/her. I pray this in Jesus's name.

14. PROMISE: "For the ways of man are before the eyes of the LORD, And He ponders all his paths" (Proverbs 5:21).

    PRAISE: Savior

    PRAYER: Our Father, cause _____ to enter in at the narrow gate, so he/she is not led to destruction (Matthew 7:13). I pray this in Jesus's name.

15. PROMISE: "And it came to pass, when Jesus had made an end of commanding his twelve disciples, he departed from thence to teach and to preach in their cities" (Matthew 11:1 KJV).

PRAISE: Omnipresent—"Where can I go from Your Spirit? Or where can I flee from Your presence? If I ascend into heaven, You are there; If I make my bed in hell, behold, You are there. If I take the wings of the morning, And dwell in the uttermost parts of the sea, Even there Your hand shall lead me, And Your right hand shall hold me" (Psalm 139:7–10).

PRAYER: Our Father, as I strive to obey the missions You've given me, please, teach and preach in my city, _____. I pray this in Jesus's name.

16. PROMISE: "The Spirit of the Lord GOD is upon Me, Because the LORD has anointed Me To preach good tidings to the poor; He has sent Me to heal the brokenhearted, To proclaim liberty to the captives, And the opening of the prison to those who are bound" (Isaiah 61:1).

PRAISE: El Shaddai, Almighty, All-Sufficient God

PRAYER: LORD, I ask You to preach good tidings to _____, heal his/her broken heart, proclaim liberty to him/her, and open his/her prison doors. I pray this in Jesus's name.

17. PROMISE: "What do you think? If a man has a hundred sheep, and one of them goes astray, does he not leave the ninety-nine and go to the mountains to seek the one that is straying? And if he should find it, assuredly, I say to you, he rejoices more over that sheep than over the ninety-nine that did not go astray. Even so it is not the will of your Father who is in heaven that one of these little ones should perish" (Matthew 18:12–14).

PRAISE: Jehovah Raah, The Lord Our Shepherd

PRAYER: Our Father, like the shepherd went to find the one lost sheep, seek _____, find him/her, and save him/her. I pray this in Jesus's name.

18. PROMISE: "For I will contend with him who contends with you, And I will save your children" (Isaiah 49:25).

PRAISE: Jehovah Nissi, The Lord Our Banner

PRAYER: Our Father, "Let the groaning of the prisoner come before You; According to the greatness of Your power Preserve those who are appointed to die" (Psalm 79:11). I pray this in Jesus's name.

19. PROMISE: "Now He who searches the hearts knows what the mind of the Spirit is, because He makes intercession for the saints according to the will of God" (Romans 8:27).

PRAISE: Omniscient, all-knowing

PRAYER: Our Father, help _____ to keep his/her heart with all diligence (Proverbs 4:23). I pray this in Jesus's name.

20. PROMISE: "For God has committed them all to disobedience, that He might have mercy on all" (Romans 11:32).

PRAISE: Merciful

PRAYER: Our Father, reveal Your mercy to _____ and grant him/her salvation that only comes from You (Psalm 85:7). I pray this in Jesus's name.

21. PROMISE: "There are many devices in a man's heart; nevertheless the counsel of the LORD, that shall stand" (Proverbs 19:21 KJV).

    PRAISE: Truth and merciful

    PRAYER: Our Father, show _____ that one day with You is better than a thousand days anywhere else. I ask that he/she will prefer to guard the door of Your house than to dwell where wickedness lives (Psalm 84:10). I pray this in Jesus's name.

22. PROMISE: "the word of the truth of the gospel, which has come to you, as it has also in all the world, and is bringing forth fruit" (Colossians 1:5–6).

    PRAISE: Word

    PRAYER: Our Father, I pray in Jesus's name that _____ will speak truth and declare righteousness (Proverbs 12:17).

23. PROMISE: "He has delivered us from the power of darkness and conveyed us into the kingdom of the Son of His love, in whom we have redemption through His blood, the forgiveness of sins" (Colossians 1:13–14).

    PRAISE: Deliverer

    PRAYER: Our Father, in Jesus's name deliver _____ from the power of darkness and translate him/her into the kingdom of Your Son.

24. PROMISE: "Are they not all ministering spirits, sent forth to minister for them who shall be heirs of salvation?" (Hebrews 1:14 KJV).

PRAISE: Jehovah Sabaoth, Lord Of Hosts, Commander of the armies of heaven

PRAYER: Our Father, I pray that _____ will inherit salvation. Please send Your angels with swords drawn to fight for him/her and to minister to him/her. Give Your angels charge over _____ to keep him/her in all of his/her ways (Psalm 91:11). I pray this in Jesus's name.

25. PROMISE: "For as the rain comes down, and the snow from heaven, And do not return there, But water the earth, And make it bring forth and bud, That it may give seed to the sower And bread to the eater, So shall My word be that goes forth from My mouth; It shall not return to Me void, But it shall accomplish what I please, And it shall prosper in the thing for which I sent it" (Isaiah 55:10–11).

PRAISE: Omniscient, all-knowing

PRAYER: Our Father, I pray _____ will fully know Your will with complete wisdom and spiritual understanding, walk worthy of You, please You always, see results in all of his/her good works, and increase in his/her knowledge of You (Colossians 1:9–10). I pray this in Jesus's name.

26. PROMISE: "so the Lord GOD will cause righteousness and praise to spring forth before all the nations" (Isaiah 61:11 KJV).

PRAISE: Jehovah Tsidkenu, The Lord Our Righteousness

PRAYER: Our Father, I pray in Jesus's name that _____ will be "filled with the fruits of righteousness, which are by Jesus Christ, unto the glory and praise of God" (Philippians 1:11 KJV).

27. PROMISE: "I will call upon the LORD, who is worthy to be praised: so shall I be saved from mine enemies" (Psalm 18:3 KJV).

    PRAISE: The living God; Jehovah, Self-Existent One, I AM

    PRAYER: Our Father, I pray in Jesus's name that _____ will long for Your courts, and that his/her heart and flesh will cry out for You, the living God (Psalm 84:2).

28. PROMISE: "This is the word of the LORD to Zerubbabel: 'Not by might nor by power, but by My Spirit,' Says the LORD of hosts" (Zechariah 4:6).

    PRAISE: Omnipotent, all-powerful God

    PRAYER: Our Father, You helped David rescue the lambs from the mouths of the lion and the bear (1 Samuel 17:34–35). Please, send someone to _____ and help that person to rescue him/her from Satan, who only roars LIKE a lion. In Jesus's name I pray.

29. PROMISE: "For I know the thoughts that I think toward you, says the LORD, thoughts of peace and not of evil, to give you a future and a hope" (Jeremiah 29:11).

    PRAISE: Jehovah Shalom, The Lord Our Peace

PRAYER: Our Father, Satan has lied to _____ about who You are and what You will or will not do. Reveal truth to him/her and cause him/her to really know that You only think thoughts of peace and not of evil toward him/her. Father, cause my prodigal to desire that hope and future You have planned for him/her and move him/her to pray to You, asking You for that future. Help him/her to know You will listen. Move _____ to search for You with all his/her heart so he/she will find You. I pray this in Jesus's name.

30. PROMISE: "Unto Adam also and to his wife did the LORD God make coats of skins, and clothed them" (Genesis 3:21 KJV). God shed the blood of animals to cover Adam and Eve. He still covers sins of sons and daughters. "Blessed is he whose transgression is forgiven, Whose sin is covered" (Romans 4:7).

    PRAISE: Jesus is our Savior—"In whom we have redemption through his blood, even the forgiveness of sins" (Colossians 1:14 KJV).

    PRAYER: Our Father, grant _____ redemption and forgiveness of sins through the blood of Your Son, Jesus. I pray in His name.

PRAY-ER ENCOURAGEMENT: When something happens that makes you feel like the situation with your prodigal is hopeless, remember you have placed your *this* in God's hands, and that is the safest place for it to be. However, when you feel burdened, pray until you feel the peace and rest return, and then remember Who is at work. God has this!

JULY

HE IS FAITHFUL

God has this. He is Faithful. We can trust Him.

The Bible is full of the faithfulness of God.

- Faithful is His name. "I saw heaven opened, and behold a white horse; and he that sat upon him was called Faithful and True" (Revelation 19:11 KJV). It's who He is!
- He will never shirk responsibility. He will never default on a promise. He will not give slack or half-hearted effort. "The Lord is not slack concerning his promise, as some men count slackness; but is longsuffering to us-ward, not willing that any should perish, but that all should come to repentance" (2 Peter 3:9 KJV).
- He is faithful to His Word. He is faithful to His name. He is faithful to who He is. He is faithful to His promises to us. He cannot and will not deny Himself. "If we are faithless, He remains faithful; He cannot deny Himself" (2 Timothy 2:13). He cannot help but to be faithful, because that is what He is and who He is. He will not deny His faithful Self, even if we do not believe. He is Faithful!
- He will never lie because He cannot lie (Titus 1:2). "Therefore know that the LORD your God, He is God, the faithful God who keeps covenant and mercy for a thousand generations with those who love Him and keep His commandments" (Deuteronomy

7:9). If God has made promises to you regarding your prodigal, you can trust that it will happen, because He cannot lie.

There are so many other verses about the faithfulness of God.

- "Great is Your faithfulness" (Lamentations 3:23).
- "He who calls you is faithful, who also will do it" (1 Thessalonians 5:24).
- "But the Lord is faithful, who will establish you and guard you from the evil one" (2 Thessalonians 3:3).
- "Your faithfulness endures to all generations" (Psalm 119:90).

When you read, "And it shall come to pass, that before they call, I will answer" (Isaiah 65:24 KJV), believe it.

When you read, "And also the Strength of Israel will not lie nor repent: for he is not a man, that he should repent" (1 Samuel 15:29 KJV), know it is true.

When the promise is, "Then I will teach transgressors Your ways, And sinners shall be converted to You" (Psalm 51:13), expect the ones you teach to be converted.

When the Bible says, "And they that heard it said, Who then can be saved? And he said, The things which are impossible with men are possible with God" (Luke 18:26–27 KJV), know that no prodigal is too far gone.

When the day's promise is, "Who shall separate us from the love of Christ? shall tribulation, or distress, or persecution, or famine, or nakedness, or peril, or sword?" (Romans 8:35 KJV), count on God to always love your prodigal.

As you read the promises each day, know that what God has promised, He will do. He is Faithful.

Remember: God has this. He is Faithful. We can trust Him.

1. PROMISE: "God is not a man, that He should lie, Nor a son of man, that He should repent. Has He said, and will He not do? Or has He spoken, and will He not make it good? Behold, I have received a command to bless; He has blessed, and I cannot reverse it" (Numbers 23:19–20).

PRAISE: He is a God of truth—"He is the Rock, his work is perfect: for all his ways are judgment: a God of truth and without iniquity; just and right is he" (Deuteronomy 32:4 KJV).

PRAYER: Our Father, when You give a promise for blessing, it will not be reversed, so we stand on Your promise and pray that You will bless _____, be merciful to him/her, and make Your face to shine upon him/her and us (Psalm 67:1). I pray this in Jesus's name.

2. PROMISE: "The Lord is not slack concerning his promise, as some men count slackness; but is longsuffering to us-ward, not willing that any should perish, but that all should come to repentance" (2 Peter 3:9 KJV).

   PRAISE: Savior

   PRAYER: Our Father, I pray that _____ will repent and be converted, that his/her sins may be blotted out, "when times of refreshing shall come from the presence of the Lord" (Acts 3:19). I pray this in Jesus's name.

3. PROMISE: "Therefore know that the LORD your God, He is God, the faithful God who keeps covenant and mercy for a thousand generations with those who love Him and keep His commandments" (Deuteronomy 7:9).

   PRAISE: Adonai, Lord and Master

   PRAYER: Our Father, "Let Your work appear to Your servants, and Your glory to their children" (Psalm 90:16). I pray this in Jesus's name.

4. PROMISE: "And you know in all your hearts and in all your souls that not one thing has failed of all the good things which the LORD your God spoke concerning you. All have come to pass for you; not one word of them has failed" (Joshua 23:14).

PRAISE: Promise Keeper

PRAYER: Our Father, I pray that _____ will forget the things in his/her past and reach forward to those things which You have ahead for him/her (Philippians 3:13). I pray this in Jesus's name.

5. PROMISE: "And also the Strength of Israel will not lie nor repent: for he is not a man, that he should repent" (1 Samuel 15:29 KJV).

PRAISE: El-Shaddai, Almighty, All-Sufficient God

PRAYER: Our Father, I pray that _____ will give heed to the things he/she has heard of and from You, and that he/she will not neglect Your great salvation (Hebrews 2:1, 3). I pray this in Jesus's name.

6. PROMISE: "There has not failed one word of all His good promise" (1 Kings 8:56).

PRAISE: Author and Finisher of faith

PRAYER: Our Father, I pray that _____ will look unto Jesus, Your Son, the author and finisher of faith (Hebrews 12:2). I pray this in Jesus's name.

7. PROMISE AND PRAISE: "And I said: 'I pray, LORD God of heaven, O great and awesome God, You who keep Your covenant and mercy with those who love You and observe Your commandments'" (Nehemiah 1:5).

    PRAYER: Our Father, I pray that _____ will fear You, walk in all Your ways, love You, serve You with all his/her heart and soul, and keep Your commandments and statutes (Deuteronomy 10:12–13). I pray this in Jesus's name.

8. PROMISE: "Let us hold fast the profession of our faith without wavering; (for he is faithful that promised)" (Hebrews 10:23 KJV).

    PRAISE: Promise Keeper

    PRAYER: Our Father, You've promised that Your Word will not return to You void, that it will prosper in what You send it to do (Isaiah 55:11), and I believe Your promises. Please, do not let Satan take away the word sown in _____'s heart. Cause his/her heart to be good ground to receive Your word and not stony, and cause Your word to take root. Do not allow persecution or tribulation to cause him/her to stumble, nor allow the cares of this world, the deceitfulness of riches, and the lusts of other things to enter in and choke Your word from his/her heart (Mark 4:15–17, 19). I pray this in Jesus's name.

9. PROMISE: "For I have said, 'Mercy shall be built up forever; Your faithfulness You shall establish in the very heavens'" (Psalm 89:2).

    PRAISE: Merciful

PRAYER: Our Father, I pray in Jesus's name that Your mercies will come to _____, and Your salvation, just as Your word promised. (Psalm 119:41).

10. PROMISE: "O LORD God of hosts, Who is mighty like You, O LORD? Your faithfulness also surrounds You" (Psalm 89:8).

PRAISE: Faithful

PRAYER: Our Father, I pray that _____ will fear You and keep Your commandments. You are faithful, and I ask that he/she will be faithful to You. In Jesus's name I pray.

11. PROMISE: "He has remembered His mercy and His faithfulness to the house of Israel; All the ends of the earth have seen the salvation of our God" (Psalm 98:3).

PRAISE: Immutable, never-changing

PRAYER: Our Father, please increase _____ in wisdom and stature and in favor with God and man, as Jesus did while He was on earth (Luke 2:52). I pray this in Jesus's name.

12. PROMISE: "For the LORD is good; His mercy is everlasting, And His truth endures to all generations" (Psalm 100:5).

PRAISE: Merciful and Truth

PRAYER: Our Father, cause _____ to not allow himself/herself to be forsaken by mercy and truth. I pray he/she will keep mercy and truth close and in his/her heart (Proverbs 3:3). I pray this in Jesus's name.

13. PROMISE: "Nevertheless he saved them for his name's sake, that he might make his mighty power to be known" (Psalm 106:8 KJV).

    PRAISE: Jehovah, Self-Existent One, Lord, Lord God

    PRAYER: Our Father, save _____ for Your name's sake. I pray this in Jesus's name.

14. PROMISE: "Your faithfulness endures to all generations" (Psalm 119:90).

    PRAISE: Merciful and gracious

    PRAYER: Our Father, I ask in Jesus's name that _____ will come boldly to the throne of grace and obtain mercy and grace (Hebrews 4:16).

15. PROMISE: "The grass withers, the flower fades, But the word of our God stands forever" (Isaiah 40:8).

    PRAISE: Immutable, never-changing

    PRAYER: Our Father, Your word promises that it will stand forever. I believe Your word that _____ has heard, read, and memorized will stand, and I am asking that Your word will light his/her path back to You (Psalm 119:105). I pray this in Jesus's name.

16. PROMISE: "And I will make an everlasting covenant with them, that I will not turn away from them, to do them good; but I will put my fear in their hearts, that they shall not depart from me" (Jeremiah 32:40 KJV).

PRAISE: Promise Keeper

PRAYER: Our Father, cause _____ to fear and serve You with all his/her heart in truth and to think on the amazing things You have done for him/her. I pray this in Jesus's name.

17. PROMISE: "And I prayed to the LORD my God, and made confession, and said, 'O Lord, great and awesome God, who keeps His covenant and mercy with those who love Him, and with those who keep His commandments" (Daniel 9:4).

PRAISE: Faithful

PRAYER: Our Father, thank You for the promise that You will keep covenant with me, because I love You and keep your commandments. I pray _____ will love and know You, for You are love (1 John 4:8). I pray this in Jesus's name.

18. PROMISE: "Therefore it is of faith, that it might be by grace; to the end the promise might be sure to all the seed; not to that only which of is the law, but to that also which is of the faith of Abraham; who is the father of us all" (Romans 4:16 KJV).

PRAISE: Father

PRAYER: Our Father, bring _____ back to his/her own border, back to You, his/her Father (Jeremiah 31:17). I pray this in Jesus's name.

19. PROMISE: "God is faithful, by whom you were called into the fellowship of His Son, Jesus Christ our Lord" (1 Corinthians 1:9).

PRAISE: Faithful Father

PRAYER: Our Father, cause _____ to "see what is the fellowship of the mystery" (Ephesians 3:9). I pray this in Jesus's name.

20. PROMISE: "No temptation has overtaken you except such as is common to man; but God is faithful, who will not allow you to be tempted beyond what you are able, but with the temptation will also make the way of escape, that you may be able to bear it" (1 Corinthians 10:13).

PRAISE: Faithful

PRAYER: Our Father, I pray that when _____ is tempted to sin, that he/she will find the way of escape and take it. I pray he/she will hate the sin in his/her life and turn to you for forgiveness. I pray this in Jesus's name.

21. PROMISE: "He who calls you is faithful, who also will do it" (1 Thessalonians 5:24).

PRAISE: God

PRAYER: Our Father, cause _____ to fear You so that You will teach him/her in the way You choose (Psalm 25:12). You are God, so teach him/her to do Your will. In pray this in Jesus's name.

22. PROMISE: "If we are faithless, He remains faithful; He cannot deny Himself" (2 Timothy 2:13).

PRAISE: Faithful

PRAYER: Our Father, I pray _____ will walk by faith, not by sight (2 Corinthians 5:7). I pray this in Jesus's name.

23. PROMISE: "If we confess our sins, he is faithful and just to forgive us our sins, and to cleanse us from all unrighteousness" (1 John 1:9 KJV).

    PRAISE: The Lord is the horn of my salvation. "The LORD is my rock, and my fortress, and my deliverer; my God, my strength, in whom I will trust; my buckler, and the horn of my salvation, and my high tower" (Psalm 18:2 KJV). The horn of salvation is a term of strength!

    PRAYER: Our Father, cause _____ to confess his/her sins, and cleanse him/her from all unrighteousness. I pray this in Jesus's name.

24. PROMISE: "Forever, O LORD, Your word is settled in heaven" (Psalm 119:89).

    PRAISE: Omnipotent, all-powerful God

    PRAYER: Our Father, I pray in Jesus's name that _____ will know nothing is too hard for You.

25. PROMISE: "For since the beginning of the world Men have not heard nor perceived by the ear, Nor has the eye seen any God besides You, Who acts for the one who waits for Him" (Isaiah 64:4).

    PRAISE: El Elyon, God Most High

PRAYER: Our Father, cause _____ to hear and to know for himself/herself that Jesus is the Christ, Your Son, and his/her Savior. I pray this in Jesus's name.

26. PROMISE: "The LORD has appeared of old to me, saying: 'Yes, I have loved you with an everlasting love; Therefore with lovingkindness I have drawn you'" (Jeremiah 31:3).

PRAISE: El Olam, Everlasting God

PRAYER: Our Father, thank You for loving _____ with Your everlasting love. Cause him/her to know what real love is and looks like (1 Corinthians 13:4–8). Draw him/her back to You. I pray in Jesus's name.

27. PROMISE: "For though I spoke against him, I earnestly remember him still; Therefore My heart yearns for him; I will surely have mercy on him, says the LORD" (Jeremiah 31:20).

PRAISE: Merciful

PRAYER: Our Father, thank You for remembering and yearning for _____. Have mercy on him/her in Jesus's name.

28. PROMISE: "For thus says the LORD GOD: 'Indeed I Myself will search for My sheep and seek them out'" (Ezekiel 34:11).

PRAISE: Jehovah Raah, The Lord Our Shepherd

PRAYER: Our Father, I pray _____ will be the sheep of Your pasture (Psalm 100:3). I pray this in Jesus's name.

29. PROMISE: "Then the nations which are left all around you shall know that I, the LORD, have rebuilt the ruined places and planted what was desolate. I, the LORD, have spoken it, and I will do it" (Ezekiel 36:36).

PRAISE: Jehovah, Self-Existent One, Lord

PRAYER: Our Father, set Your eyes on _____ for good and bring him/her back to You. Build _____ and don't pull him/her down. Plant _____ and don't pull him/her up. Give him/her a heart to know You, that You are the LORD. Cause him/her to return to You with his/her whole heart so he/she can be Yours and You will be his/her God (Jeremiah 24:6-7). I pray this in Jesus's name.

30. PROMISE: "The word of God is not bound" (2 Timothy 2:9 KJV).

PRAISE: Defense

PRAYER: Our Father, I pray You will cause the counsel of the nations and people's plans to have no effect in _____'s life and Your counsel and plans to stand forever for him/her and all of his/her descendants (Psalm 33:10–11). I pray this in Jesus's name.

31. PROMISE: "For He spoke, and it was done; He commanded, and it stood fast" (Psalm 33:9).

PRAISE: Sovereign

PRAYER: Our Father, I pray Your word may run swiftly and be glorified in _____ (2 Thessalonians 3:1). I pray this in Jesus's name.

PRAY-ER ENCOURAGEMENT: God is faithful. Your faith doesn't make Him that way, and your doubt doesn't change Him. When a circumstance with your prodigal causes your faith to falter, come back to this chapter and read through the promises. Let them rebuild your faith or increase your measure of faith for the first time (Romans 12:3). And remember: God has this; He is Faithful; You can trust Him!

Tami Winkelman

AUGUST

WE CAN TRUST HIM

Have you ever felt like God let you down? Sometimes it may seem like it, but He has never let you down, and nor will He ever. He is Faithful, so we can trust Him.

The Bible reminds us: "As for God, his way is perfect; the word of the LORD is tried: he is a buckler to all them that trust in him" (2 Samuel 22:31 KJV). God has this; He is Faithful; we can trust Him!

Psalm 118:8 tells us "It is better to trust in the LORD than to put confidence in man" (KJV).

- Trust Him as Jehovah Tsidkenu, The Lord Our Righteousness, to give you His righteousness so your prayers can be heard and effective.
- Trust Him as Savior to forgive your prodigal.
- Trust Him as Jehovah Rapha, The Lord Our Healer, to heal your prodigal.
- Trust Him as omniscient, all-knowing God, and as Father to do what is best for your prodigal.
- Trust Him as Jehovah Nissi, The Lord Our Banner, to be victorious in your battle for your prodigal and in your prodigal's battle; to plant His standard in his/her life, claiming him/her as His own; and to bring your prodigal to dwell under His ensign. "… but as for me and my house, we will serve the LORD" (Joshua 24:15 KJV).

- Trust Him as El Olam, Everlasting God, to love your prodigal with His everlasting love.
- Trust Him as omnipresent God, who is not only present in all places, but also in all times, to know what to promise you because He already exists in the future and knows what is happening there.
- Trust Him as Jehovah Sabaoth, Lord Of Hosts, Commander of the armies of heaven, to send His warrior angels with swords drawn to fight for your prodigal and you.
- Trust Him as El Elyon, God Most High, to outrank every enemy.
- Trust Him as Jehovah Shammah, The Lord Is There, to always be with your prodigal, to never leave or forsake him/her.
- Trust Him as Jehovah M'Kaddesh, The Lord Who Sanctifies, to sanctify your prodigal, to set him/her apart, and to prepare him/her for service.
- Trust Him as immutable, unchangeable God to keep His promises to you, because His word does not change.
- Trust Him as a just God to always do the right thing by your prodigal.
- Trust Him as Jehovah Jireh, The Lord Our Provider, to be able to provide whatever your prodigal needs.
- Trust Him as El Shaddai, Almighty, All-Sufficient God, to be able to overcome the enemy of your prodigal and to grant grace sufficient for your prodigal's needs.
- Trust Him as El, God Of Power And Might, to be able to handle whatever you entrust to Him.
- Trust Him as Jehovah Raah, The Lord Our Shepherd, to lead your prodigal in the way he/she should go.
- Trust Him as Jehovah Shalom, The Lord Our Peace, to not only speak peace to your prodigal but to you as you wait.

It may seem at times that your prodigal's *this* is too big for God, but it isn't. If your prodigal is a murderer, a rapist, an atheist, an agnostic, a liar, a thief, an addict, a prostitute, isolated from you, lazy, rude, foul-mouthed, homeless, a morally good person, or any other thing a prodigal can be, we can trust Him to reach him or her. God can handle it. He can reach your prodigal.

Remember from last month: "Let us hold fast the profession of our faith without wavering; (for he is faithful that promised)" (Hebrews 10:23 KJV).

God has this. He is Faithful. We can trust Him.

1. PROMISE AND PRAISE: "The LORD is my rock, and my fortress, and my deliverer; my God, my strength, in whom I will trust; my buckler, and the horn of my salvation, and my high tower. I will call upon the LORD, who is worthy to be praised: so shall I be saved from mine enemies" (Psalm 18:2–3 KJV).

   PRAYER: Our Father, I pray in Jesus's name that _____ will call upon You in the day of trouble, that You will deliver him/her, and that he/she will glorify You.

2. PROMISE: "Some trust in chariots, and some in horses: but we will remember the name of the LORD our God" (Psalm 20:7 KJV).

   PRAISE: "The name of the LORD is a strong tower; The righteous run to it and are safe" (Proverbs 18:10).

   PRAYER: God of _____'s salvation, help him/her. Deliver him/her for Your glory and the sake of Your name (Psalm 79:9). I pray this in Jesus's name.

3. PROMISE: "Our soul waits for the LORD; He is our help and our shield. For our heart shall rejoice in Him, Because we have trusted in His holy name" (Psalm 33:20–21).

   PRAISE: Deliverer and Shield

PRAYER: Our Father, deliver _____ from evil, and keep him/her from evil. I pray this in Jesus's name.

4. PROMISE: "Oh, taste and see that the LORD is good; Blessed is the man who trusts in Him!" (Psalm 34:8).

    PRAISE: Good

    PRAYER: Our Father, I pray _____ will trust in You at all times and pour out his/her heart before You (Psalm 62:8). I pray this in Jesus's name.

5. PROMISE: "He who dwells in the secret place of the Most High Shall abide under the shadow of the Almighty. I will say of the LORD, 'He is my refuge and my fortress; My God, in Him I will trust.' Surely He shall deliver you from the snare of the fowler And from the perilous pestilence. He shall cover you with His feathers, And under His wings you shall take refuge; His truth shall be your shield and buckler. You shall not be afraid of the terror by night, Nor of the arrow that flies by day" (Psalm 91:1–5).

    PRAISE: El Elyon, God Most High

    PRAYER: Our Father, I pray _____ will live in the secret place of the Most High and abide in the shadow of the Almighty, make You his/her refuge and fortress, and trust in You. I pray You will deliver him/her from the snare of the fowler and from the perilous pestilence. Protect him/her, and do not let him/her be afraid of the terror by night. I pray this in Jesus's name.

6. PROMISE: "The LORD is merciful and gracious, slow to anger, and plenteous in mercy" (Psalm 103:8 KJV).

PRAISE: Merciful

PRAYER: Our Father, I am so grateful You are merciful, gracious, and slow to anger. Holy Spirit, convict _____ of sin, because he/she says he/she does not believe in You. I pray this in Jesus's name.

7. PROMISE: "You who fear the LORD, trust in the LORD; He is their help and their shield" (Psalm 115:11).

PRAISE: Adonai, Lord and Master

PRAYER: Our Father, I pray that _____ will listen to You, and that You will teach him/her to fear You (Psalm 34:11). I pray this in Jesus's name.

8. PROMISE: "Among the gods there is none like You, O Lord; Nor are there any works like Your works" (Psalm 86:8).

PRAISE: El Elyon, God Most High

PRAYER: Our Father, I pray _____ will not allow himself/herself to be deceived by spirits and demon's doctrines, speak hypocritical lies, or have his/her "conscience seared with a hot iron" (1 Timothy 4:1–2 KJV). In Jesus's name I pray.

9. PROMISE: "But Jesus beheld them, and said unto them, With men this is impossible; but with God all things are possible" (Matthew 19:26 KJV).

PRAISE: Able

PRAYER: Our Father, I pray in Jesus's name that _____'s faith would "not stand in the wisdom of men but in" Your power (1 Corinthians 2:5 KJV).

10. PROMISE: "The LORD is good to all: and his tender mercies are over all his works. ... The LORD is righteous in all his ways, and holy in all his works" (Psalm 145:9, 17 KJV).

PRAISE: Good

PRAYER: Our Father, I noticed the word *all* in this promise, and I am thankful my prodigal is included in Your *all*. Cause _____ to understand the way of Your precepts and meditate on Your wonderful works (Psalm 119:27). I pray this in Jesus's name.

11. PROMISE: "This is the LORD; we have waited for him, we will be glad and rejoice in His salvation" (Isaiah 25:9 KJV).

PRAISE: Savior

PRAYER: Our Father, I pray in Jesus's name that _____ will "take the helmet of salvation" (Ephesians 6:17 KJV).

12. PROMISE: "Have you not known? Have you not heard? The everlasting God, the LORD, The Creator of the ends of the earth, Neither faints nor is weary. His understanding is unsearchable" (Isaiah 40:28).

PRAISE: Elohim, Triune God, Creator

PRAYER: Our Father, I praise You as creative God. I love knowing that Your methods of reaching _____ are better than anything I could even imagine. I pray in Jesus's name that You will show _____ the path of life and help him/her know that full and everlasting joy can only be found in Your presence (Psalm 16:11).

13. PROMISE: "Ah Lord GOD! Behold, You have made the heavens and the earth by Your great power and outstretched arm. There is nothing too hard for You" (Jeremiah 32:17).

PRAISE: El, God Of Power And Might

PRAYER: Our Father, command the light to shine into _____'s dark heart "to give the light of the knowledge of the glory of God in the face of Jesus Christ" (2 Corinthians 4:6 KJV). I pray this in Jesus's name.

14. PROMISE: "And being fully persuaded that, what he had promised, he was also able to perform" (Romans 4:21 KJV).

PRAISE: Redeemer

PRAYER: Our Father, cause _____ to "put on the new man, which after God is created in righteousness and true holiness" (Ephesians 4:24 KJV). I pray this in Jesus's name.

15. PROMISE: "What shall we then say to these things? If God be for us, who can be against us?" (Romans 8:31 KJV).

PRAISE: Omnipotent, all-powerful

PRAYER: Our Father, cause _____ to listen to You so he/she can dwell in safety and "be quiet from fear of evil" (Proverbs 1:33 KJV). I pray this in Jesus's name.

16. PROMISE: "He that spared not his own Son, but delivered him up for us all, how shall he not with him also freely give us all things?" (Romans 8:32 KJV).

    PRAISE: Jehovah M'Kaddesh, The Lord Who Sanctifies

    PRAYER: Our Father, I pray that _____, who is separated from You and in his/her mind is presently an enemy of Your kingdom because of his/her wicked works, would be reconciled to You (Colossians 1:21). I pray this in Jesus's name.

17. PROMISE: "O the depth of the riches both of the wisdom and knowledge of God! how unsearchable are his judgments, and his ways past finding out!" (Romans 11:33 KJV).

    PRAISE: Wise

    PRAYER: Our Father, I ask You to send someone often to remind _____ of truth and wise ways, and that he/she will receive godly wisdom freely. I pray _____ will not harden his/her neck so he/she will not be destroyed (Proverbs 29:1). Cause my prodigal to hear life's rebukes and "abide among the wise." (Proverbs 15:31). In Jesus's name I pray.

18. PROMISE: "For all the promises of God in Him are Yes, and in Him Amen, to the glory of God through us" (2 Corinthians 1:20).

    PRAISE: Promise Keeper

    PRAYER: Our Father, remind _____ that Your promises are Yes and Amen and that You are true to Your word and Your word is true. I pray this in Jesus's name.

19. PROMISE: "In Him you also trusted, after you heard the word of truth, the gospel of your salvation; in whom also, having believed, you were sealed with the Holy Spirit of promise, who is the guarantee of our inheritance until the redemption of the purchased possession, to the praise of His glory" (Ephesians 1:13–14).

PRAISE: Truth

PRAYER: Our Father, _____ has heard the word of truth, the gospel of Your salvation. Cause him/her to trust in You through that word and be saved and sealed with the Holy Spirit of promise. I pray this in Jesus's name.

20. PROMISE: "But God, who is rich in mercy, because of His great love with which He loved us, even when we were dead in trespasses, made us alive together with Christ (by grace you have been saved)" (Ephesians 2:4–5).

PRAISE: Love

PRAYER: Our Father, show _____ Your great love for him/her, and make him/her alive with Christ. I pray this in Jesus's name.

21. PROMISE: "Therefore He is also able to save to the uttermost those who come to God through Him, since He always lives to make intercession for them" (Hebrews 7:25).

PRAISE: Intercessor

PRAYER: Jesus, save _____ to the uttermost. Thank You for always making intercession for him/her. I pray this in Jesus's name.

22. PROMISE: "For the LORD God is a sun and shield: the LORD will give grace and glory: no good thing will he withhold from them who walk uprightly" (Psalm 84:11 KJV).

PRAISE: Gracious

PRAYER: Our Father, the good thing I am asking is that _____ will choose the way of truth. I pray this in Jesus's name.

23. PROMISE: "And the LORD passed by before him and proclaimed, The LORD, the LORD God, merciful and gracious, longsuffering, and abundant in goodness and truth, Keeping mercy for thousands, forgiving iniquity and transgression and sin" (Exodus 34:6–7 KJV).

PRAISE: Merciful

PRAYER: Our Father, have mercy on _____, according to Your lovingkindness; according to the multitude of Your tender mercies, blot out his/her transgressions (Psalm 51:1). I pray this in Jesus's name.

24. PROMISE: "For the Lord will not cast off forever. Though He causes grief, Yet He will show compassion According to the multitude of His mercies. For He does not afflict willingly, Nor grieve the children of men" (Lamentations 3:31–33).

PRAISE: Jehovah Nissi, The Lord Our Banner

PRAYER: "Lord, how long will You look on? Rescue [_____] from their destructions" (Psalm 35:17). I will thank and praise You. I pray this in Jesus's name.

25. PROMISE: "As a shepherd seeks out his flock on the day he is among his scattered sheep, so will I seek out My sheep and deliver them from all the places where they were scattered on a cloudy and dark day" (Ezekiel 34:12).

PRAISE: Jehovah Raah, The Lord Our Shepherd

PRAYER: Our Father, I pray in Jesus's name that You will seek out _____ and deliver him/her from all the dark places the enemy has taken him/her.

26. PROMISE: "So I will restore to you the years that the swarming locust has eaten" (Joel 2:25).

PRAISE: Adonai, Lord and Master

PRAYER: Our Father, save _____, and restore the years the locust has eaten. Pour out Your Spirit on him/her. I pray this in Jesus's name.

27. PROMISE: "You are a gracious and merciful God, slow to anger and abundant in lovingkindness, One who relents from doing harm" (Jonah 4:2).

PRAISE: Gracious and merciful

PRAYER: Restore _____, O God of our salvation, and cause Your anger toward him/her to cease (Psalm 85:4). I pray this in Jesus's name.

28. PROMISE: "That your faith should not stand in the wisdom of men, but in the power of God" (1 Corinthians 2:5 KJV).

PRAISE: Omnipotent, all-powerful God

PRAYER: Our Father, I pray in Jesus's name that _____ will "Beware lest anyone cheat [him/her] through philosophy and empty deceit, according to the tradition of men, according to the basic principles of the world, and not according to Christ" (Colossians 2:8).

29. PROMISE: "As far as the east is from the west, So far has He removed our transgressions from us" (Psalm 103:12).

    PRAISE: Jehovah M'Kaddesh, The Lord Who Sanctifies

    PRAYER: Our Father, wash _____, and he/she shall be whiter than snow (Psalm 51:7). I pray this in Jesus's name.

30. PROMISE: "But the Comforter, which is the Holy Ghost, whom the Father will send in my name, he shall teach you all things, and bring all things to your remembrance, whatsoever I have said unto you" (John 14:26 KJV).

    PRAISE: Holy Spirit, Helper

    PRAYER: Our Father, do not let Your sayings depart from _____'s ears and eyes, and cause him/her to keep those promises in the midst of his/her heart (Proverbs 4:20–21). I pray this in Jesus's name.

31. PROMISE: "However, when He, the Spirit of truth, has come, He will guide you into all truth; for He will not speak on His own authority, but whatever He hears He will speak; and He will tell you things to come" (John 16:13).

PRAISE: Truth

PRAYER: Our Father, we know this promise is not only true for prodigals, but when Your Spirit tells us things to come, we can know they will happen. Holy Spirit, guide _____ into all truth so the truth will set him/her free (John 8:32). I pray this in Jesus's name.

PRAY-ER ENCOURAGEMENT: When you don't know what to do, "Trust in the LORD with all your heart, And lean not on you own understanding; In all your ways acknowledge Him, And He shall direct your paths" (Proverbs 3:5–6). When you need peace, remember: "You will keep him in perfect peace, Whose mind is stayed on You, Because he trusts in You" (Isaiah 26:3). When you need strength, "Trust in the LORD forever, For in YAH, the LORD, is everlasting strength" (Isaiah 26:4). When there is trouble all around, hold on to the fact that "God is our refuge and strength, a very present help in trouble" (Psalm 46:1 KJV). And remember: God has this; He is Faithful; you can trust Him!

SEPTEMBER

MIND THE GAP

Mind the gap. Mind the gap. Mind the gap.

We were in London and frequently rode the Tube. "The gap" refers to the small space between the train floor and the platform. The reminder seemed to be everywhere: over the intercom and on T-shirts, refrigerator magnets, signs, and posters.

Why were there constant reminders? Had someone been hurt because they did not mind the gap?

Well, someone has been hurt because of the gap between God and man: the prodigal.

The Bible addresses this gap. Ezekiel 22:30 says, "So I sought for a man among them who would make a wall, and stand in the gap before Me on behalf of the land, that I should not destroy it; but I found no one."

We can be diligent to mind the gap for our prodigal through prayer, inviting God to change a heart, heal a hurt, save a soul, deliver from the evil one, reveal a truth, expose a lie, send an angel with sword drawn to fight for our prodigals, send a laborer into the harvest field of our prodigals, and whatever else God lays on our hearts to pray.

Mind the gap. Who else will be as diligent as you?

1. PROMISE: "Oh, fear the LORD, you His saints! There is no want to those who fear Him" (Psalm 34:9).

PRAISE: Adonai, Lord and Master

PRAYER: Our Father, I do fear You. My *want* is that You completely wash _____ from iniquity and sin (Psalm 51:2). I pray this in Jesus's name.

2. PROMISE: "The eyes of the LORD are upon the righteous, and his ears are open unto their cry" (Psalm 34:15 KJV).

    PRAISE: Jehovah Tsidkenu, The Lord Our Righteousness

    PRAYER: Our Father, thank You for making me righteous so You can hear my prayer. My heart's cry is that _____ will "walk not after the flesh, but after the Spirit" (Romans 8:4 KJV). I pray this in Jesus's name.

3. PROMISE: "The righteous cry out, and the LORD hears, And delivers them out of all their troubles" (Psalm 34:17).

    PRAISE: Deliverer

    PRAYER: Our Father, I pray in Jesus's name that You deliver _____ "from the way of evil, From the man who speaks perverse things" (Proverbs 2:12).

4. PROMISE: "And let the beauty of the LORD our God be upon us, And establish the work of our hands for us; Yes, establish the work of our hands" (Psalm 90:17).

    PRAISE: Truth

    PRAYER: Our Father, I worked diligently to make sure _____ knows Your word and about You. I pray in Jesus's name that You will establish that work and that he/she will hear and keep the instruction of his/her father and mother (Proverbs 1:8).

5. PROMISE: "Because he has set his love upon Me, therefore I will deliver him; I will set him on high, because he has known My name. He shall call upon Me, and I will answer him; I will be with him in trouble; I will … show him My salvation" (Psalm 91:14–16).

PRAISE: El Shaddai, Almighty, All-Sufficient God

PRAYER: Our Father, _____ has known Your name in the past. I pray that _____ will believe in You and love You, even though he/she has not physically seen You, and receive the salvation of his/her soul. Cause him/her to rejoice with unspeakable joy (1 Peter 1:8). I pray this in Jesus's name.

6. PROMISE: "I will lift up my eyes to the hills—From whence comes my help? My help comes from the LORD, Who made heaven and earth" (Psalm 121:1–2).

PRAISE: Help

PRAYER: Lord, as our salvation, quickly help _____ (Psalm 38:22). I pray this in Jesus's name.

7. PROMISE: "Blessed be the LORD my Rock, Who trains my hands for war, And my fingers for battle" (Psalm 144:1).

PRAISE: Jehovah Nissi, The Lord Our Banner

PRAYER: Our Father, we are fighting for _____ through prayer, as You have required. Cause him/her to not enter the path of the wicked, nor walk in the way of evil men. I pray he/she will avoid it and not travel on it, but turn from it and pass on (Proverbs 4:14–15). I pray this in Jesus's name.

8. PROMISE: "The LORD is nigh unto all them that call upon him, to all that call upon him in truth. He will fulfil the desire of them that fear him" (Psalm 145:18–19 KJV).

   PRAISE: Jehovah, Self-Existent One

   PRAYER: Our Father, my heart's desire is for _____ to be saved. Cause him/her to fear You and hate evil. I pray this in Jesus's name.

9. PROMISE: "Behold, the eye of the LORD is upon them that fear him, upon them that hope in his mercy" (Psalm 33:18 KJV).

   PRAISE: Veil-Ripper!—"Then the veil of the temple was torn in two from top to bottom" (Mark 15:38).

   PRAYER: Our Father, when the blind man cried out to You, You asked what he wanted You to do for him. "And he said, Lord, that I may receive my sight," and You made him see (Luke 18:35–42 KJV). Lord, what I want You to do for me is to make _____ see You and lift the veil of deception so he/she can see truth. I pray this in Jesus's name.

10. PROMISE: "while I was speaking in prayer, the man Gabriel, whom I had seen in the vision at the beginning, being caused to fly swiftly, reached me about the time of the evening offering. And he informed me, and talked with me, and said, 'O Daniel, I

have now come forth to give you skill to understand. At the beginning of your supplications the command went out, and I have come to tell you, for you are greatly beloved'" (Daniel 9:21–23). The answer to Daniel's prayer began the minute he prayed.

PRAISE: Jehovah Sabaoth, Lord Of Hosts, Commander of the armies of heaven

PRAYER: Our Father, You sent Gabriel in answer to Daniel's prayer, and I ask that You will send Your holy angels to fight for _____. I pray this is Jesus's name.

11. PROMISE: "Therefore I will look unto the LORD; I will wait for the God of my salvation: my God will hear me" (Micah 7:7 KJV).

    PRAISE: Jehovah M'Kaddesh, The Lord Who Sanctifies

    PRAYER: Our Father, perfect that which concerns _____. Thank You that Your mercy endures forever. Please, do not forsake him/her, the work of Your own hands (Psalm 138:8). I pray this in Jesus's name.

12. PROMISE: "Ask, and it will be given to you; seek, and you will find; knock, and it will be opened to you. For everyone who asks receives, and he who seeks finds, and to him who knocks it will be opened" (Matthew 7:7–8).

    PRAISE: The Way

    PRAYER: Our Father, I stand on this promise. I am asking You in Jesus's name to cause _____ to seek You with all of his/her heart and help him/her to find You (Jeremiah 29:13). Thank You for answering this prayer.

13. PROMISE: "Or what man is there among you who, if his son asks for bread, will give him a stone? Or if he asks for a fish, will he give him a serpent? If you then, being evil, know how to give good gifts to your children, how much more will your Father who is in heaven give good things to those who ask Him!" (Matthew 7:9–11).

PRAISE: Jehovah Jireh, The Lord Who Will See To It

PRAYER: Our Father, I pray in Jesus's name that _____ will have the fruit of the Spirit: love, joy, peace, longsuffering, gentleness, goodness, faith, meekness, temperance (Galatians 5:22–23).

14. PROMISE: "Assuredly, I say to you, whatever you bind on earth will be bound in heaven, and whatever you loose on earth will be loosed in heaven" (Matthew 18:18).

PRAISE: Deliverer—"Therefore if the Son makes you free, you shall be free indeed" (John 8:36).

PRAYER: Our Father, I pray in Jesus's name that every evil spirit hindering _____'s salvation and his/her return to You be stopped and every evil plan against him/her destroyed, and that he/she will be set free.

15. PROMISE: "When Jesus saw their faith, He said to the paralytic, 'Son, your sins are forgiven you'" (Mark 2:5).

PRAISE: Light

PRAYER: Our Father, when Jesus saw the faith of those carrying the paralytic, He saved him. I ask that You see my faith in Your promise regarding _____, and that he/she will come to the light and be forgiven of his/her evil deeds. I pray against this tendency to stay away from the light and that he/she will love light rather than darkness (John 3:19–20). I pray this in Jesus's name.

16. PROMISE: In Mark 9:19–27, a dad brings his son to Jesus to be delivered of a spirit, and Jesus delivers him. The last two verses of this story say: "many said, 'He is dead.' But Jesus took him by the hand and lifted him up, and he arose."

    PRAISE: Jesus is Life—"Jesus said to him, 'I am the way, the truth, and the life. No one comes to the Father except through Me'" (John 14:6).

    PRAYER: Our Father, I see _____'s life deteriorating, so I bring him/her to You and ask that You stop the thief from stealing, killing, and destroying him/her, and give him/her the abundant life You have provided (John 10:10). I pray this in Jesus's name.

17. PROMISE: "So they said, 'Believe on the Lord Jesus Christ, and you will be saved, you and your household'" (Acts 16:31).

    PRAISE: Deliverer

    PRAYER: Our Father, I do believe in You and am trusting this promise. In this passage of Scripture, the opening of the prison doors for Paul and Silas caused the keeper of the prison to ask what he must do to be saved. You know if it will take a miracle to move _____ to ask what he/she needs to do to be saved.

Father, please, allow him/her to witness that miracle and save him/her. I pray this in Jesus's name.

18. PROMISE: "For everyone who asks receives, and he who seeks finds, and to him who knocks it will be opened" (Luke 11:10).

PRAISE: Mighty

PRAYER: Our Father, I pray _____ will cleanse his/her hands, purify his/her heart, and no longer be double-minded (James 4:8). I pray this in Jesus's name.

19. PROMISE: "But this is what was spoken by the prophet Joel: 'And it shall come to pass in the last days, says God, That I will pour out of My Spirit on all flesh; Your sons and your daughters shall prophesy, Your young men shall see visions, Your old men shall dream dreams. … And it shall come to pass That whoever calls on the name of the LORD Shall be saved'" (Acts 2:16–17, 21).

PRAISE: Holy Spirit

PRAYER: Our Father, pour out of Your Spirit on _____, and cause him/her to prophesy and see visions. I pray he/she will call on Your name and be saved. In Jesus's name I pray.

20. PROMISE: "Your prayers and your alms have come up for a memorial before God" (Acts 10:4).

PRAISE: Jehovah Raah, The Lord Our Shepherd

PRAYER: Our Father, like you sent Peter to the house of Cornelius, please, send someone to witness to _____ to move him/her to salvation. I pray this in Jesus's name.

21. PROMISE: "And the hand of the Lord was with them: and a great number believed, and turned to the Lord" (Acts 11:21 KJV).

PRAISE: Redeemer

PRAYER: Our Father, I know Your hand is with me, and I pray that _____ will believe, turn to You, and be a new creation in Your Son, and that old things will pass away and all things will become new (2 Corinthians 5:17). I pray this in Jesus's name.

22. PROMISE: "Likewise the Spirit also helps in our weaknesses. For we do not know what we should pray for as we ought, but the Spirit Himself makes intercession for us with groanings which cannot be uttered" (Romans 8:26).

PRAISE: Deliverer

PRAYER: Our Father, I ask that You send Your Holy Spirit to help _____ do no evil (2 Corinthians 13:7), and that he/she would be delivered by You from evil men (Psalm 140:1). I also ask, Holy Spirit, that when I do not know how I should pray that You make intercession for _____. I pray this in Jesus's name.

23. PROMISE: "Now all things are of God, who has reconciled us to Himself through Jesus Christ, and has given us the ministry of reconciliation" (2 Corinthians 5:18).

PRAISE: Redeemer

PRAYER: Our Father, You have given me the ministry of reconciliation, as well as to others around _____. Cause the love of godly people around him/her to be without hypocrisy. Cause him/her to abhor things that are evil and to cling to things that are good (Romans 12:9). I pray this in Jesus's name.

24. PROMISE: "God was in Christ reconciling the world to Himself, not imputing their trespasses to them, and has committed to us the word of reconciliation" (2 Corinthians 5:19).

PRAISE: Guide

PRAYER: "O LORD, I know the way of man is not in himself; It is not in man who walks to direct his own steps." Correct _____ justly but not in Your anger, so that he/she will not be brought to nothing (Jeremiah 10:23-24). I pray this in Jesus's name.

25. PROMISE: "And let us not be weary in well doing: for in due season we shall reap, if we faint not" (Galatians 6:9 KJV).

PRAISE: Deliverer

PRAYER: Our Father, I pray _____ will "escape the snare of the devil," who has taken him/her captive to do his will (2 Timothy 2:26). I pray this in Jesus's name.

26. PROMISE: "Therefore do not cast away your confidence, which has great reward. For you have need of endurance, so that after

you have done the will of God, you may receive the promise: 'For yet a little while, And He who is coming will come and will not tarry'" (Hebrews 10:35–37).

PRAISE: Jehovah Shalom, The Lord Our Peace

PRAYER: Our Father, I believe I will receive Your promises to me regarding _____, and I pray in Jesus's name that he/she will "let the peace of God rule in" his/her heart (Colossians 3:15 KJV).

27. PROMISE: "Brethren, if anyone among you wanders from the truth, and someone turns him back, let him know that he who turns a sinner from the error of his way will save a soul from death and cover a multitude of sins" (James 5:19–20).

PRAISE: Revealer

PRAYER: Our Father, my prodigal is in opposition to You. I pray in Jesus's name that You will send someone to _____ who will humbly correct him/her, and that You will grant him/her repentance so he/she will know the truth (2 Timothy 2:25).

28. PROMISE: "when I call to remembrance the genuine faith that is in you, which dwelt first in your grandmother Lois and your mother Eunice, and I am persuaded is in you also" (2 Timothy 1:5).

PRAISE: Guide

PRAYER: Our Father, help _____ to keep his/her father's commands, to not forsake the law of his/her mother, and to bind them continually upon his/her heart, so when he/she roams, they will lead him/her (Proverbs 6:20–22). I pray this in Jesus's name.

29. PROMISE: "If anyone sees his brother sinning a sin which does not lead to death, he will ask, and He will give him life for those who commit sin not leading to death" (1 John 5:16).

PRAISE: Life

PRAYER: Our Father, please cause _____ to put off the old man and be renewed in the spirit of his mind (Ephesians 4:22–23). I pray You will give him/her life in Jesus's name.

30. PROMISE: "Now when He had taken the scroll, the four living creatures and the twenty-four elders fell down before the Lamb, each having a harp, and golden bowls full of incense, which are the prayers of the saints" (Revelation 5:8).

PRAISE: Able

PRAYER: Our Father, in this promise Your word says our prayers stay before Your throne, and I am grateful to know my prayers for _____ are there. Now I ask that _____ put his/her prayers there, being "anxious for nothing, but in everything by prayer and supplication, with thanksgiving," make his/her requests known to You (Philippians 4:6). I pray this in Jesus's name.

PRAY-ER ENCOURAGEMENT: People who love prodigals rarely have to be reminded to pray for them, but there are times of discouragement that can grow into a sense of futility. Even if we have feelings of hopelessness or have thoughts that praying may be useless, we still pray, and when we do not know what else to pray, the Holy

Spirit will make intercession for the situation. God will soon restore our faith, and we can know He is working, whether we can see it or not. We still love our prodigals, and we still mind the gap!

OCTOBER

CIRCUMSTANCES DO NOT CHANGE THE PROMISE

"(For we walk by faith, not by sight)" (2 Corinthians 5:7 KJV).

God prepared me.

It is a personal goal each day to read at least one verse of Jesus's words, the red words, in the morning and before bed. One morning as I prepared to take my morning walk, I felt God pulling me to read the red *before* my walk. The verse I read that morning was Mark 5:39 in the King James Version: "Why make ye this ado, and weep? the damsel is not dead, but sleepeth." The New King James Version reads, "Why make this commotion and weep? The child is not dead, but sleeping."

Jesus's words are always important, but when I read them that morning, I did not know just how much help they would soon be to me, but my heavenly Father knew I would need them. I walked out of my door, stepped onto the driveway, and met face to face with evidence that challenged God's promises to me regarding a prodigal. The many raindrops, the overwhelming evidence of prayers answered, suddenly seemed insignificant. Before this horrible moment, I had witnessed progress. Now all territory taken back from Satan *seemed* lost.

My normal response to such a moment would have been to panic. My mind would paint a picture of the worst-case scenario, and I would usually begin praying intensely, begging God and trying to manipulate Him into doing things a better way, *my* definition of better.

A few seconds into my working up a frenzy, I remembered God's personal promise to me moments before. He had prepared me, so why was I making a commotion? Many, many prayers had gone to the throne of God for this prodigal, and God had answered them—and in probably more ways than I was even aware. I *knew* He had this. I *knew* He is faithful. I *knew* I could trust Him.

The life of someone praying for a prodigal is full of ups and downs. You pray until you come to a place of total trust and faith in the promise, and then something happens that shakes you to your core. If we focus on our surroundings or the circumstances involved in the lives of our prodigals, our faith can plummet. However, we must keep our mind on the promise, because that is what is true.

God knew about our tendency to focus on what we can see and hear. Perhaps that is why He had Paul write these words: "Finally, brethren, whatsoever things are true, whatsoever things are honest, whatsoever things are just, whatsoever things are pure, whatsoever things are lovely, whatsoever things are of good report; if there be any virtue, and if there be any praise, think on these things" (Philippians 4:8 KJV).

When your faith seems weakened for the moment, meditate on this verse: "God is not a man, that He should lie, Nor a son of man, that He should repent. Has He said, and will He not do? Or has He spoken, and will He not make it good?" (Numbers 23:19). This verse fits the protocol: it is true, honest, just, pure, lovely, of good report, virtuous, and praiseworthy just as Paul pointed out in his letter to the Philippians.

I am tired of relearning lessons God has already shown me, even if the lapse is only for a few minutes. When I am slapped in the face with a new circumstance or doubt, I want to immediately go into faith mode, Scripture-quoting mode, praise mode. God did promise to make the crooked straight and the mountains and valleys flat (Isaiah 40:4). He can make these ups and downs to be the same: times of faith and trusting in Him.

There will be times when God burdens me to pray for my prodigal, but I do not want to ever fall into frantic moments because of a lie from Satan. I believe God will do this for me.

There is no reason to panic or make a commotion! Our prodigals are not dead, but only sleeping.

1. PROMISE: "For His anger is but for a moment, His favor is for life; Weeping may endure for a night, But joy comes in the morning" (Psalm 30:5).

   PRAISE: Longsuffering and merciful

   PRAYER: Our Father, cause _____ to hear Your lovingkindness in the morning and to put his/her trust in You (Psalm 143:8). I pray this in Jesus's name.

2. PROMISE: "Now may the God of hope fill you with all joy and peace in believing, that you may abound in hope by the power of the Holy Spirit" (Romans 15:13).

   PRAISE: God of hope

   PRAYER: God of hope, fill _____ with all joy and peace in believing, that he/she may have an abundance of hope by the Holy Spirit's power. I pray this in Jesus's name.

3. PROMISE: "With him is strength and wisdom: the deceived and the deceiver are his" (Job 12:16 KJV).

   PRAISE: Omnipotent and wise

   PRAYER: Our Father, _____ is deceived, and he/she is Yours. Deliver him/her "from lying lips, and from a deceitful tongue" (Psalm 120:2 KJV). I pray this in Jesus's name.

4. PROMISE: "Good and upright is the LORD; Therefore He teaches sinners in the way" (Psalm 25:8).

   PRAISE: Good—God is completely good.

PRAYER: Our Father, hear in heaven and forgive _____'s sin. Show him/her how to walk in Your good way. I pray this in Jesus's name.

5. PROMISE: "The counsel of the LORD stands forever, The plans of His heart to all generations" (Psalm 33:11).

   PRAISE: Wise

   PRAYER: Our Father, instruct and guide _____ and teach him/her the best way to go. I pray this in Jesus's name.

6. PROMISE: "And my soul shall be joyful in the LORD: it shall rejoice in his salvation" (Psalm 35:9 KJV).

   PRAISE: Savior

   PRAYER: Our Father, please visit _____ with Your salvation and cause him/her to "see the benefit of Your chosen ones" and to "glory with Your inheritance" (Psalm 106:4–5). I pray this in Jesus's name.

7. PROMISE: "You have with Your arm redeemed Your people" (Psalm 77:15).

   PRAISE: Redeemer

   PRAYER: Our Father, I believe the promises You have given me for _____'s salvation and that it is as good as done. He/she is Yours. I will still be faithful to ask for Your will to be done in earth. Redeem him/her from the hand of the enemy. I pray this in Jesus's name.

8. PROMISE: "If his children forsake my law, and walk not in my judgments; If they break my statutes, and keep not my commandments; Then will I visit their transgression with the rod, and their iniquity with stripes. Nevertheless my lovingkindness will I not utterly take from him, nor suffer my faithfulness to fail. My covenant will I not break, nor alter the thing that is gone out of my lips" (Psalm 89:30–34 KJV).

PRAISE: Adonai, Lord and Master

PRAYER: Our Father, I pray _____ will submit to You, resist the devil so he will flee, draw near to You so You will draw near to him/her, cleanse his/her hands, and purify his/her heart (James 4:7-8). I pray this in Jesus's name.

9. PROMISE: "For the LORD will not cast off his people, neither will he forsake his inheritance" (Psalm 94:14 KJV).

PRAISE: Father—"I will be a Father to you, And you shall be My sons and daughters, Says the LORD Almighty" (2 Corinthians 6:18).

PRAYER: Our Father, I pray against the spirit of bondage in _____ and pray that he/she will receive the Spirit of adoption so he/she can cry out to You as his/her Father (Romans 8:15). I pray this in Jesus's name.

10. PROMISE: "Where can I go from Your Spirit? Or where can I flee from Your presence?" (Psalm 139:7).

PRAISE: Omnipresent, present in all places and in all times

PRAYER: Our Father, like Adam and Eve hid themselves from You in their sin, _____ is doing the same thing: hiding from You and other godly influences. I pray against isolation in his/her life in Jesus's name.

11. PROMISE: "and that from childhood you have known the Holy Scriptures, which are able to make you wise for salvation through faith which is in Christ Jesus" (2 Timothy 3:15).

PRAISE: Truth

PRAYER: Our Father, _____ has known the Holy Scriptures from childhood. He/she has erred in spirit and complained about his/her upbringing (Isaiah 29:24). Cause the Scriptures to make him/her wise for salvation through faith which is in Christ Jesus. I pray this in Jesus's name.

12. PROMISE: "They wandered in the wilderness in a solitary way; they found no city to dwell in. Hungry and thirsty, their soul fainted in them. Then they cried unto the LORD in their trouble, and he delivered them out of their distresses" (Psalm 107:4–6 KJV).

PRAISE: Jehovah Shalom, The Lord Our Peace

PRAYER: Our Father, I pray _____ will be spiritually minded so he/she can have life and peace (Romans 8:6). I pray this in Jesus's name.

13. PROMISE: "If I ascend into heaven, You are there; If I make my bed in hell, behold, You are there" (Psalm 139:8).

PRAISE: Omnipresent, present in all times and all places

PRAYER: Our Father, no matter where _____ goes, I pray that he/she will know You are with him/her. Cause Your presence to draw him/her back to You. I pray this in Jesus's name.

14. PROMISE: "If I say, 'Surely the darkness shall fall on me,' Even the night shall be light about me; Indeed, the darkness shall not hide from You, But the night shines as the day; The darkness and the light are both alike to You" (Psalm 139:11–12).

    PRAISE: Light

    PRAYER: Our Father, illuminate the darkness around and in _____. I pray this in Jesus's name.

15. PROMISE: "A man's heart plans his way, But the LORD directs his steps" (Proverbs 16:9).

    PRAISE: Guide

    PRAYER: Our Father, many times _____'s plans do not reflect Your purpose for his/her life, but I find comfort in knowing that You will direct his/her steps no matter the plans he/she makes. So that is my prayer today: even though his/her heart plans the way, that You would direct his/her steps. Let Your purpose reign. I pray this in Jesus's name.

16. PROMISE: "Who has performed and done it, Calling the generations from the beginning? 'I, the LORD, am the first; And with the last I am He'" (Isaiah 41:4).

    PRAISE: El Olam, Everlasting God

PRAYER: Our Father, You have a purpose for _____ , and I believe that purpose will be fulfilled, but Satan is robbing him/her of this time with You. Save _____ and restore to him/her and to Your kingdom those things lost, and doubly anoint him/her for his/her work in Your kingdom in Jesus's name.

17. PROMISE: "Saying to a tree, 'You are my father,' And to a stone, 'You gave birth to me.' For they have turned their back to Me, and not their face. But in the time of their trouble they will say, 'Arise and save us'" (Jeremiah 2:27).

PRAISE: Elohim, Triune God, Creator

PRAYER: Our Father, this is a trap into which many prodigals fall. I pray that _____ will know that YOU created him/her and that he/she is not a product of evolution. Help him/her choose to serve You above all other gods (Joshua 24:15). In Jesus's name I pray.

18. PROMISE: "To the Lord our God belong mercies and forgiveness, though we have rebelled against him" (Daniel 9:9 KJV).

PRAISE: Jehovah Tsidkenu, The Lord Our Righteousness

PRAYER: Our Father, You know _____'s secret faults. Cleanse him/her from them. Keep him/her away from presumptuous sins, and do not let them rule over him/her (Psalm 19:12-13). I pray this in Jesus's name.

19. PROMISE: "Who shall separate us from the love of Christ? shall tribulation, or distress, or persecution, or famine, or nakedness, or peril, or sword?" (Romans 8:35 KJV).

PRAISE: Love

PRAYER: Our Father, root and ground _____ in love that he/she may be able to comprehend the width, length, depth, and height of Your love (Ephesians 3:17–19). I pray this in Jesus's name.

20. PROMISE: "For I am persuaded, that neither death, nor life, nor angels, nor principalities, nor powers, nor things present, nor things to come, Nor height, nor depth, nor any other creature, shall be able to separate us from the love of God, which is in Christ Jesus our Lord" (Romans 8:38–39 KJV).

PRAISE: Love

PRAYER: Our Father, direct _____'s heart into the love of God (2 Thessalonians 3:5). I pray this in Jesus's name.

21. PROMISE: "'With a little wrath I hid My face from you for a moment; But with everlasting kindness I will have mercy on you,' Says the LORD, your Redeemer" (Isaiah 54:8).

PRAISE: Redeemer

PRAYER: Our Father, give _____ hope, and cause him/her to know that he/she can be redeemed, forgiven. Cause him/her to call on You for salvation. Be merciful to _____, a sinner, as You were to the tax collector (Luke 18:13). I pray this in Jesus's name.

22. PROMISE: "Then He came and touched the open coffin, and those who carried him stood still. And He said, 'Young man, I say to you, arise.' So he who was dead sat up and began to speak. And He presented him to his mother" (Luke 7:14–15).

    PRAISE: Life

    PRAYER: Our Father, as You raised the young man from Nain from death, raise _____ from spiritual death and present him/her to his/her family. I can hardly wait! I pray this in Jesus's name.

23. PROMISE: "He staggered not at the promise of God through unbelief; but was strong in faith, giving glory to God" (Romans 4:20 KJV).

    PRAISE: El Elyon, God Most High

    PRAYER: Our Father, I pray that no matter the circumstances surrounding _____ , my faith will not waver. I also pray that he/she will put his/her "affection on things above, not on things on the earth" (Colossians 3:2 KJV) and that he/she will be saved and come out of these sinful, earthly circumstances. I pray this in Jesus's name.

24. PROMISE: "But if we hope for that we see not, then do we with patience wait for it" (Romans 8:25 KJV).

    PRAISE: Jehovah Shammah, The Lord Is There—we praise Him as Jehovah Shammah, because He is in the future and knows that what He is promising will come true.

    PRAYER: Our Father, I am thankful for the promises You have given me regarding _____ . Thomas physically walked with You on Earth, saw You, and still doubted, but You met him in his unbelief, revealed Yourself to him, and gave him faith (John 20:27). _____ has walked with You and now has doubted and left the faith. Please, meet him/her where he/she is, reveal Yourself to him/her, and give him/her faith. Restore _____ to salvation. I pray this in Jesus's name.

25. PROMISE: Speaking of the prisoners and those who are in darkness, Isaiah says, "They shall neither hunger nor thirst, Neither heat nor sun shall strike them; For He who has mercy on them will lead them, Even by the springs of water He will guide them" (Isaiah 49:10).

PRAISE: Merciful

PRAYER: Our Father, bring _____ out of darkness and protect him/her. Send Your tender mercies to _____ so he/she can live. I pray this in Jesus's name.

26. PROMISE: "We are troubled on every side, yet not distressed; we are perplexed, but not in despair; Persecuted, but not forsaken; cast down, but not destroyed" (2 Corinthians 4:8–9 KJV).

PRAISE: Defense

PRAYER: Our Father, I am not praying for You to remove _____ from the world, but that You will keep him/her away from evil (John 17:15). I pray this in Jesus's name.

27. PROMISE: "For I will not contend forever, Nor will I always be angry; For the spirit would fail before Me, And the souls which I have made. For the iniquity of his covetousness I was angry

and struck him; I hid and was angry, And he went on backsliding in the way of his heart. I have seen his ways, and will heal him; I will also lead him, And restore comforts to him And to his mourners" (Isaiah 57:16–18).

PRAISE: Merciful

PRAYER: Our Father, show your mercy to _____. Yes, he/she has sinned, but Your Word says your mercies and compassions are new every morning (Lamentations 3:22–23). Keep him/her from doing anything that will hinder his/her salvation and calling, ministry, and purpose. Protect his/her mind, body, soul and spirit. Save my prodigal, Lord, in the name of Jesus.

28. PROMISE: "Then I said, I will not make mention of him, nor speak any more in his name. But his word was in mine heart as a burning fire shut up in my bones, and I was weary with forbearing, and I could not stay" (Jeremiah 20:9 KJV).

PRAISE: The Word

PRAYER: Our Father, Your word has been given, read, preached, and sung to _____. Let it be like a fire shut up in his/her bones, even if he/she has determined to not mention You or speak Your name. Make him/her weary of holding it back and cause him/her to minister as You have created him/her to do. I pray this in Jesus's name.

29. PROMISE: "And it shall come to pass, that as I have watched over them to pluck up, to break down, to throw down, to destroy, and to afflict, so I will watch over them to build" (Jeremiah 31:28).

PRAISE: Sovereign

PRAYER: Our Father, Your word promises thoughts of peace and not for evil. Please, give _____ the future for which You created him/her, and give him/her hope in You (Jeremiah 29:11). I pray this in Jesus's name.

30. PROMISE: "For the gifts and the calling of God are irrevocable" (Romans 11:29).

    PRAISE: Good

    PRAYER: Our Father, make _____ worthy of his/her calling and fulfill Your every purpose in his/her life. By Your power finish Your work of faith in _____ (2 Thessalonians 1:11). I pray this in Jesus's name.

31. PROMISE: "In Him also we have obtained an inheritance, being predestined according to the purpose of Him who works all things according to the counsel of His will" (Ephesians 1:11).

    PRAISE: Sovereign

    PRAYER: Our Father, show the mystery of Your will to _____. I pray this in Jesus's name.

PRAY-ER ENCOURAGEMENT: "Now it came to pass on a certain day, that [Jesus] went into a ship with his disciples: and he said unto them, Let us go over unto the other side of the lake" (Luke 8:22 KJV). Remember that when the Lord says, "Let us cross over unto the other side," you will make it to the other side, no matter the circumstances that come along the way. He will be with you in every part of your journey, even when you feel He is not paying attention. He is always aware of your circumstances and will see you safely to the other side if you just ask.

NOVEMBER

WE ARE WALKING IN VICTORY WHILE PRAYING THROUGH CIRCUMSTANCES

Prodigals by definition are not in a good place in their spiritual lives, and because of this, their life can include many complications, bad decisions, heartaches, heartbreaks, needs, strongholds, disappointments, etc. Witnessing the destruction can be painful to those who love them.

When we know of those times, we pray. We pray through the circumstances.

When God lays a burden on our hearts, we pray. We pray until the burden lifts.

When we are tired of the fight, we pray. We pray until we are strengthened for the fight.

When we suddenly feel anxious, we pray. We pray until we have peace.

If you are the parent or grandparent of the prodigal, your position is complicated by the love you have for them. The instincts we feel to protect them—fix-it instincts—can get in the way of the work God is wanting to do in our prodigal's life, so we have to find our place of rest. His way of protecting and fixing is always best.

When God promises, it is done—rest while praying through circumstances.

God is working—rest while praying through circumstances.

God is answering your prayers—rest while praying through circumstances.

When circumstances are hard, remember circumstances do not change the promise—rest while praying through those circumstances.

Pray. Trust God. Rest.

We are walking in the victory won on the cross, the victory promised in God's true Word, and the victory He has promised us personally. The victory is ours!

We are walking in victory while praying through the circumstances!

PRAYER FOR THANKSGIVING CELEBRATIONS: Our Father, I am grateful for my prodigal, _____, and for the hope You have given me for his/her salvation. Thank You for all that You have done and are doing in his/her life, the ones I have witnessed and the ones I have not: for drawing him/her back to Yourself, sparing his/her life, sending true Christians into his/her path as witnesses, removing ungodly influences, keeping him/her from evil and keeping evil from him/her, lifting the veil, breaking strongholds, reminding him/her of truths from Your word, giving him/her hope for salvation, and so much more.

Father, I ask that nothing will hinder _____ from joining the family for Thanksgiving celebrations. I pray You will ordain every conversation and attitude, and that there will be a mending of relationships where that is needed. Let Your love, peace, and joy be evident in the lives of Christians in the house as a witness. Let nothing be said or done that will hinder _____'s salvation and let everything bring You glory. In Jesus's name I pray. Amen.

1. PROMISE: "They that sow in tears shall reap in joy" (Psalm 126:5 KJV).

   PRAISE: Jehovah M'Kaddesh, The Lord Who Sanctifies

   PRAYER: Our Father, cause _____ to walk in the counsel of the godly, stand in the way of the righteous, and sit in the seat of the joyful. Cause him/her to delight in Your law and meditate in it day and night (Psalm 1:1–2). I pray this in Jesus's name.

2. PROMISE: "Though I walk in the midst of trouble, You will revive me; You will stretch out Your hand Against the wrath of my enemies, And Your right hand will save me. The LORD will perfect that which concerns me; Your mercy, O LORD, endures forever" (Psalm 138:7–8).

   PRAISE: Jehovah Nissi, The Lord Our Banner—God fights for those who are His.

   PRAYER: Our Father, thank You for all you have already done to bring _____ back to Yourself. He/she is walking in trouble. I pray You will revive and save him/her, come against his/her enemies, and perfect that which concerns him/her. Do not forsake the works of Your hands. In Jesus's name I pray.

3. PROMISE: "having predestined us to adoption as sons by Jesus Christ to Himself, according to the good pleasure of His will, to the praise of the glory of His grace, by which He made us accepted in the Beloved" (Ephesians 1:5–6).

   PRAISE: Father

   PRAYER: Our Father, I pray that You will cause _____ to ponder the path of his/her feet, establish all of his/her ways, and turn not to the right or the left, and that he/she will remove her foot from evil (Proverbs 4:26–27). I ask that he/she will live as Your son/daughter. I pray this in Jesus's name.

4. PROMISE: "Call upon Me in the day of trouble; I will deliver you, and you shall glorify Me" (Psalm 50:15).

PRAISE: Deliverer

PRAYER: Jesus, _____ is a prisoner, so please tell him/her to go forth. He/she is in darkness, so please tell him/her to show himself/herself (Isaiah 49:9). I pray this in Your name.

5. PROMISE: "Whoever offers praise glorifies Me; And to him who orders his conduct aright I will show the salvation of God" (Psalm 50:23).

   PRAISE: Savior

   PRAYER: Our Father, show me Your salvation in _____. "Oh, turn to me, and have mercy on me! Give Your strength to Your servant, And save the son of Your maidservant" (Psalm 86:16). I pray this in Jesus's name.

6. PROMISE: "In the day of my trouble I will call upon You, For You will answer me" (Psalm 86:7).

   PRAISE: Jehovah Nissi, The Lord Our Banner

   PRAYER: Our Father, keep _____ from walking in the way of sinners, and keep his/her foot from their path (Proverbs 1:15). I pray this in Jesus's name.

7. PROMISE: "You are my hiding place and my shield; I hope in Your word" (Psalm 119:114).

   PRAISE: Jehovah M'Kaddesh, The Lord Who Sanctifies

   PRAYER: Our Father, I pray _____ will recall the knowledge of You so he/she can receive Your exceeding great and precious promises, partake of the divine nature, and escape the corruption that is in the world through lust (2 Peter 1:3–4).

8. PROMISE: "Unless Your law had been my delight, I would then have perished in my affliction" (Psalm 119:92).

PRAISE: Word

PRAYER: Our Father, I thank You for Your word. It brings me comfort in this fight for my prodigal. I pray _____ will no longer be childish, "tossed to and fro, and carried about with every wind of doctrine, by the sleight of men, and cunning craftiness, whereby they lie in wait to deceive" (Ephesians 4:14 KJV). I pray this in Jesus's name.

9. PROMISE: "He who continually goes forth weeping, Bearing seed for sowing, Shall doubtless come again with rejoicing, Bringing his sheaves with him" (Psalm 126:6).

PRAISE: Adonai, Lord and Master

PRAYER: Our Father, we have wept over our prodigal and planted seeds into his/her life. I pray in Jesus's name that You will send laborers into the harvest field that is _____'s life (Matthew 9:38; Luke 10:2). Thank You for the promise of rejoicing and our reaping a harvest.

10. PROMISE: "to comfort all that mourn … to give unto them beauty for ashes, the oil of joy for mourning, the garment of praise for the spirit of heaviness; that they might be called trees of righteousness, the planting of the LORD, that he might be glorified" (Isaiah 61:2–3 KJV).

PRAISE: Sovereign

PRAYER: Our Father, thank You for the comfort, beauty, joy, and praise that You are working from these circumstances. _____ has gone on backsliding in the way of his/her heart. Look on _____'s ways and heal him/her. Lead my prodigal and comfort him/her and those who mourn for him/her (Isaiah 57:17–18). I pray this in Jesus's name.

11. PROMISE: "And whatever things you ask in prayer, believing, you will receive" (Matthew 21:22).

PRAISE: Omniscient, all-knowing

PRAYER: Search and try _____ and know his/her heart and thoughts to see if there is any wickedness in him/her. Guide him/her in the way that will lead to eternal life (Psalm 139:23-24). I pray this in Jesus's name.

12. PROMISE: "So shall they fear The name of the LORD from the west, And His glory from the rising of the sun; When the enemy comes in like a flood, The Spirit of the LORD will lift up a standard against him" (Isaiah 59:19).

PRAISE: Jehovah Nissi, The Lord Our Banner

PRAYER: Jehovah Nissi, plant Your ensign, Your banner, Your standard in _____. Claim him/her as Your own. Fight for him/her against the enemy of his/her soul. Give him/her the victory in every spiritual battle. I pray this in Jesus's name.

13. PROMISE: "And blessed is she that believed: for there will be a performance of those things which were told her from the Lord" (Luke 1:45 KJV).

PRAISE: Faithful

PRAYER: Our Father, I believe Your promises regarding my prodigal will be fulfilled. I pray _____ will guard what You committed to his/her trust and avoid "profane and vain babblings, and oppositions of science falsely so called" (1 Timothy 6:20 KJV). I pray this in Jesus's name.

14. PROMISE: "Rejoicing in hope; patient in tribulation; continuing instant in prayer" (Romans 12:12 KJV).

PRAISE: Adonai, Lord and Master

PRAYER: Our Father, I pray that _____ will believe that Jesus is the Son of God so he/she can overcome the world (1 John 5:4–5). I pray this in Jesus's name.

15. PROMISE: "(For we walk by faith, not by sight)" (2 Corinthians 5:7 KJV). Circumstances do not change the promise.

PRAISE: Jehovah, Self-Existent One, I AM

PRAYER: Our Father, I pray in Jesus's name that _____'s faith will grow exceedingly.

16. PROMISE: "For though we walk in the flesh, we do not war according to the flesh. For the weapons of our warfare are not carnal but mighty in God for pulling down strongholds, casting down arguments and every high thing that exalts itself against

the knowledge of God, bringing every thought into captivity to the obedience of Christ" (2 Corinthians 10:3–5).

PRAISE: Mighty

PRAYER: Our Father, help us to use the mighty weapons in You to pull down strongholds in _____'s life, cast down arguments and every high thing that exalts itself against the knowledge of You, and bring into captivity every thought in obedience to You. I pray this in Jesus's name.

17. PROMISE: "All your children shall be taught by the LORD, And great shall be the peace of your children" (Isaiah 54:13).

PRAISE: Teacher

PRAYER: Our Father, instruct _____ and teach him/her out of Your law. Give him/her rest from the days of adversity (Psalm 94:12–13). I pray this in Jesus's name.

18. PROMISE: "No weapon formed against you shall prosper, And every tongue which rises against you in judgment You shall condemn" (Isaiah 54:17).

PRAISE: Jehovah M'Kaddesh, The Lord Who Sanctifies

PRAYER: Our Father, do not let _____ sin in anger or "give place to the devil" (Ephesians 4:26–27 KJV). Father, I pray he/she will fear You, so he/she will be turned away from the snares of death (Proverbs 14:27). I pray this in Jesus's name.

19. PROMISE: "Return to the LORD your God, For He is gracious and merciful, Slow to anger, and of great kindness; And He relents from doing harm" (Joel 2:13).

PRAISE: Deliverer

PRAYER: Our Father, cause _____ to "lay aside every weight, and the sin which so easily ensnares" him/her (Hebrews 12:1). Father, please, remove every obstacle in his/her path on his/her way back to You. I pray this in Jesus's name.

20. PROMISE: "Let the wicked forsake his way, and the unrighteous man his thoughts: and let him return unto the LORD, and he will have mercy upon him; and to our God, for he will abundantly pardon" (Isaiah 55:7 KJV).

PRAISE: Omniscient, all-knowing—"'For My thoughts are not your thoughts, Nor are your ways My ways,' says, the LORD. 'For as the heavens are higher than the earth, So are My ways higher than your ways, And My thoughts than your thoughts'" (Isaiah 55:8–9).

PRAYER: Our Father, I pray in Jesus's name that _____ will forsake his/her way and thoughts and return to You. Thank You for Your mercy and pardon for him/her.

21. PROMISE: "I will cause them to walk by the rivers of waters in a straight way, wherein they shall not stumble" (Jeremiah 31:9 KJV).

PRAISE: Jehovah Tsidkenu, The Lord Our Righteousness

PRAYER: Our Father, lead _____ in the paths of righteousness for the sake of Your name. I pray this in Jesus's name.

22. PROMISE: "Who is a God like You? … He does not retain His anger forever, Because He delights in mercy" (Micah 7:18).

PRAISE: Merciful and Truth

PRAYER: Our Father, cause mercy and truth to reign in _____'s life so that his/her iniquity will be purged. I pray he/she will fear You so he/she will depart from evil. I pray this in Jesus's name.

23. PROMISE: "The thief does not come except to steal, and to kill, and to destroy. I have come that they may have life, and that they may have it more abundantly" (John 10:10).

PRAISE: Life

PRAYER: Our Father, I pray _____ will no longer live for himself/herself, but for Him who died for him/her and rose again. In Jesus's name I pray.

24. PROMISE: "I love the LORD, because He has heard My voice and my supplications. Because He has inclined His ear to me, Therefore I will call upon Him as long as I live" (Psalm 116:1–2).

PRAISE: Light

PRAYER: Our Father, it is time for _____ to wake up. Cause him/her to cast off the works of darkness and put on the armor of light (Romans 13:11–12). I pray this in Jesus's name.

25. PROMISE: "For the eyes of the Lord are over the righteous, and his ears are open unto their prayers" (1 Peter 3:12 KJV).

PRAISE: Jehovah M'Kaddesh, The Lord Who Sanctifies

PRAYER: Our Father, I pray _____ will crucify "the flesh with the affections and lusts" and will live and walk in the Spirit (Galatians 5:24–25 KJV). I pray this in Jesus's name.

26. PROMISE: "All scripture is given by inspiration of God, and is profitable for doctrine, for reproof, for correction, for instruction in righteousness: That the man of God may be perfect, thoroughly furnished unto all good works" (2 Timothy 3:16–17 KJV).

PRAISE: Word

PRAYER: Our Father, _____ has heard the word many times, and I pray that he/she will be a doer of the word, and not a hearer only, so that he/she will not be deceived (James 1:22). I pray my prodigal will be complete, thoroughly furnished unto all good works. I pray this in Jesus's name.

27. PROMISE: "For You are the glory of their strength, And in Your favor our horn is exalted" (Psalm 89:17).

PRAISE: Light—"That was the true Light which gives light to every man coming into the world" (John 1:9).

PRAYER: Our Father, our hope is in You. Bless _____, keep him/her, shine Your face on him/her, be gracious to him/her, and give him/her peace (Numbers 6:24-26). I pray this in Jesus's name.

28. PROMISE: "For they indeed for a few days chastened us as seemed best to them, but He for our profit, that we may be partakers of His holiness. Now no chastening seems to be joyful for the present, but painful; nevertheless, afterward it yields the peaceable fruit of righteousness to those who have been trained by it" (Hebrews 12:10–11).

PRAISE: Jehovah Tsidkenu, The Lord Our Righteousness

PRAYER: Our Father, I pray in Jesus's name that mercy and truth will meet together and that righteousness and peace will kiss each other in _____'s life (Psalm 85:10).

29. PROMISE: "Salvation belongs to our God who sits on the throne, and to the Lamb!" (Revelation 7:10).

PRAISE: The Way

PRAYER: Our Father, show _____ the way he/she should walk and cause him/her to lift his/her soul up to You. I pray this in Jesus's name.

30. PROMISE: "O LORD God of our fathers, are You not God in heaven, and do You not rule over all the kingdoms of the nations, and in Your hand is there not power and might, so that no one is able to withstand You?" (2 Chronicles 20:6).

PRAISE: "For unto us a child is born, unto us a son is given: and the government shall be upon his shoulder: and his name shall be called Wonderful, Counsellor, The mighty God, The everlasting Father, The Prince of Peace" (Isaiah 9:6 KJV).

PRAYER: Our Father, _____ and the enemies of his/her soul are not able to withstand You. I pray he/she will not be "overcome of evil, but overcome evil with good" (Romans 12:21 KJV). I pray this in Jesus's name.

PRAY-ER ENCOURAGEMENT: When circumstances are dire and hope is bleak, pray and hold onto the promises of God. Believe them and walk in victory while you pray your prodigal through the circumstances of life that come from bad, sinful choices. And remember: circumstances do not change the promise!

DECEMBER

HOPE

The first time I saw my babies, I absorbed with awe the perfection of the creation of God: every little thing in the right place, every detail, down to the hairs on their heads numbered by God.

The God who created them so beautifully actually came to Earth as a baby Himself to grow up and pay our debt owed because of sin. He became our Emmanuel. He became our hope.

At the end of each day, in the midst of difficulties or in a calm, we have hope because of who God is and what Christ did.

Over and over again, the Bible says that evil men face punishment for their wickedness. The descriptions of those wicked men fit prodigals in so many ways. This breaks our hearts, but we know that the situation is not hopeless. We have hope in God. They have hope in God. We ask God to rescue them from the wicked way, to redeem them, to save them from a life of sin. We put them in His capable-to-the-extreme hands where hope lies.

These two verses describe us as we wait:

- "But if we hope for that we see not, then do we with patience wait for it" (Romans 8:25 KJV).
- "Rejoicing in hope; patient in tribulation; continuing instant in prayer" (Romans 12:12 KJV).

We are thankful for the hope we have in Emmanuel. During this Christmas season, pray that the message and hope of Christ will take

147

root in the heart of your prodigal, and then rest in the hope of God's saving grace.

"Happy is he who has the God of Jacob for his help, Whose hope is in the LORD his God" (Psalm 146:5).

PRAYER FOR CHRISTMAS CELEBRATIONS: Our Father, I love _____ with my whole heart, and I thank You for him/her and the promises You have given me. I praise You as sovereign Lord! I ask that You ordain our family times and not allow anything to hinder our time together. Ordain our conversation. Use me to bless but not preach, to love but not smother, and to be used by You and not try to control or change things myself or in my own version of wisdom. I pray that our home will be flooded with peace and joy that only comes from You and that it will remind _____ of the peace and joy that results from being in right relationship with You, causing him/her to long for that again. I also pray that the effects of sin that I witness will not throw me into distress but will simply move me to pray in total faith, committing it all to you, knowing that You have this, You are Faithful, and I can trust You. In Jesus's name I pray. Amen.

1. PROMISE: "every way, whether in pretense, or in truth, Christ is preached" (Philippians 1:18 KJV).

    PRAISE: Emmanuel, God With Us

    PRAYER: Our Father, the message of Christmas is everywhere: in pulpits, on Christian and secular radio, in stores by people who want our money, on billboards, in magazines, etc., but one thing remains: the gospel is being spread, no matter their motive. I pray _____ will be taught by You and know the truth that is in Jesus (Ephesians 4:21). I pray this in Jesus's name.

2. PROMISE: "He has made everything beautiful in its time. Also He has put eternity in their hearts" (Ecclesiastes 3:11).

PRAISE: El Olam, Everlasting God—"Before the mountains were brought forth, Or ever You had formed the earth and the world, Even from everlasting to everlasting, You are God" (Psalm 90:2).

PRAYER: Our Father, sanctify _____ by the truth of Your word (John 17:17), and give him/her a desire to spend eternity with You. In Jesus's name I pray.

3. PROMISE: "I shall not die, but live, and declare the works of the LORD" (Psalm 118:17 KJV).

    PRAISE: Able

    PRAYER: Our Father, I ask that _____ will keep Your commands and live (Proverbs 7:2). I pray this in Jesus's name.

4. PROMISE: "For I will pour water on him who is thirsty, And floods on the dry ground; I will pour My Spirit on your descendants, And My blessing on your offspring; They will spring up among the grass Like willows by the watercourses" (Isaiah 44:3–4).

    PRAISE: Holy Spirit

    PRAYER: Our Father, _____ is my descendant, my offspring. This promise is wonderful to him/her! Please, pour Your living water, Your Spirit, and Your blessing on him/her. I pray this in Jesus's name.

5. PROMISE: "Thus says the LORD: 'In an acceptable time I have heard You, And in the day of salvation I have helped You; I will preserve You and give You As a covenant to the people, To

restore the earth, To cause them to inherit the desolate heritages; That You may say to the prisoners, "Go forth," To those who are in darkness, "Show yourselves"" (Isaiah 49:8–9).

PRAISE: Father

PRAYER: Our Father, make _____ Your son/daughter instead of a slave of Satan, and Your heir (Galatians 4:7). I pray this in Jesus's name.

6. PROMISE: "Can a woman forget her nursing child, And not have compassion on the son of her womb? Surely they may forget, Yet I will not forget you. See, I have inscribed you on the palms of My hands; Your walls are continually before Me. Your sons shall make haste" (Isaiah 49:15–17).

PRAISE: Jehovah Tsidkenu, The Lord Our Righteousness

PRAYER: Our Father, for Your name's sake revive _____, and because of Your righteousness bring his/her soul out of trouble. I pray this in Jesus's name.

7. PROMISE: "Then you shall know that I am the LORD, when I have opened your graves, O My people, and brought you up from your graves" (Ezekiel 37:13).

PRAISE: Life

PRAYER: Our Father, You restored the son of the Shunammite woman. Please, restore _____ to Yourself and breathe life back into him/her (2 Kings 4:34-36). I pray this in Jesus's name.

8. PROMISE: "'As for Me,' says the LORD, 'this is My covenant with them: My Spirit who is upon you, and My words which I have put in your mouth, shall not depart from your mouth, nor from the mouth of your descendants, nor from the mouth of your descendants' descendants,' says the LORD, 'from this time and forevermore'" (Isaiah 59:21).

    PRAISE: Word

    PRAYER: Our Father, I pray _____ will let the word of Christ dwell in himself/herself richly in all wisdom (Colossians 3:16 KJV). I pray this in Jesus's name.

9. PROMISE: "'Do I have any pleasure at all that the wicked should die?' says the Lord GOD, 'and not that he should turn from his ways and live?'" (Ezekiel 18:23).

    PRAISE: Friend

    PRAYER: Our Father, show _____ that "friendship of the world is enmity with" You (James 4:4 KJV), and cause him/her to want to be Your friend rather than the world's. I pray this in Jesus's name.

10. PROMISE: "So God created man in his own image, in the image of God created he him; male and female created he them" (Genesis 1:27 KJV).

    PRAISE: Jehovah Raah, The Lord Our Shepherd

    PRAYER: Our Father, move _____ to "walk in the way of good men, and keep the paths of the righteous" (Proverbs 2:20 KJV). I pray this in Jesus's name.

11. PROMISE: "Then Peter said to them, 'Repent, and let every one of you be baptized in the name of Jesus Christ for the remission of sins; and you shall receive the gift of the Holy Spirit. For the promise is to you and to your children, and to all who are afar off, as many as the Lord our God will call'" (Acts 2:38-39).

PRAISE: Holy Spirit

PRAYER: Our Father, cause _____ to believe, and seal him/her with the Holy Spirit of promise (Ephesians 1:13). I pray this in Jesus's name.

12. PROMISE: "Be of good courage, And He shall strengthen your heart, All you who hope in the LORD" (Psalm 31:24).

PRAISE: God of hope

PRAYER: Our Father, forget _____'s past iniquities. Quickly send Your tender mercies to help him/her, because he/she is in a very low place (Psalm 79:8). I pray this in Jesus's name.

13. PROMISE: "The people who walked in darkness Have seen a great light; Those who dwelt in the land of the shadow of death, Upon them a light has shined" (Isaiah 9:2).

PRAISE: Light

PRAYER: Our Father, I pray _____, who is walking in darkness and dwells in the shadow of death, will see a great light. Increase his/her joy and cause him/her to rejoice before You. I pray this in Jesus's name.

14. PROMISE: "Behold, I will bring them from the north country, and gather them from the coasts of the earth, and with them the blind and the lame" (Jeremiah 31:8 KJV).

    PRAISE: Redeemer

    PRAYER: Our Father, please grant to _____ that he/she can come to Jesus (John 6:65). I pray this in Jesus's name.

15. PROMISE: "There is hope in your future, says the LORD, That your children shall come back to their own border" (Jeremiah 31:17).

    PRAISE: Jehovah Tsidkenu, The Lord Our Righteousness

    PRAYER: Our Father, lead _____ into the land of uprightness (Psalm 143:10 KJV). I pray this in Jesus's name.

16. PROMISE: "'The LORD is my portion,' says my soul, 'Therefore I hope in Him!' The LORD is good to those who wait for Him, To the soul who seeks Him. It is good that one should hope and wait quietly For the salvation of the LORD" (Lamentations 3:24–26).

    PRAISE: God of hope

    PRAYER: Our Father, cause _____ to say, "The LORD is my portion therefore I hope in Him!" I pray this in Jesus's name.

17. PROMISE: "And the God of peace shall bruise Satan under your feet shortly. The grace of our Lord Jesus Christ be with you. Amen" (Romans 16:20 KJV).

PRAISE: Omniscient

PRAYER: Our Father, make _____ "wise unto that which is good, and simple concerning evil" (Romans 16:19 KJV). I pray this in Jesus's name.

18. PROMISE: "For the vision is yet for an appointed time, but at the end it shall speak, and not lie: though it tarry, wait for it; because it will surely come, it will not tarry" (Habakkuk 2:3 KJV).

PRAISE: Jehovah Shammah, The Lord Is There

PRAYER: Our Father, I pray _____ will seek You while You may be found and call upon You while You are near (Isaiah 55:6). In Jesus's name I pray.

19. PROMISE: "And she will bring forth a Son, and you shall call His name JESUS, for He will save His people from their sins" (Matthew 1:21).

PRAISE: The way, truth, and life

PRAYER: Our Father, cause _____ to KNOW that Jesus is THE way, THE truth, and THE life, and not just a possibility or just a good man (John 14:6). I pray this in Jesus's name.

20. PROMISE: "For the Son of man is come to seek and to save that which was lost" (Luke 19:10 KJV).

PRAISE: Savior

PRAYER: Our Father, _____ is lost, but the promise in Luke is one the best promises. You saved Zacchaeus that day; please seek and save _____, I pray, in Jesus's name.

21. PROMISE: "Happy is he who has the God of Jacob for his help, Whose hope is in the LORD his God" (Psalm 146:5).

    PRAISE: Hope

    PRAYER: Our Father, I pray in Jesus's name that _____ will set his/her hope in You and not forget Your works, but keep Your commandments.

22. PROMISE: "And they shall come from the east, and from the west, and from the north, and from the south, and shall sit down in the kingdom of God" (Luke 13:29 KJV).

    PRAISE: El Shaddai, Almighty, All-Sufficient God

    PRAYER: Our Father, Your word says, "No one can come to Me unless the Father who sent Me draws him; and I will raise him up at the last day" (John 6:44). I ask, Father, that You will draw _____, and that he/she will sit down in Your kingdom. Thank You for this promise. I pray this in Jesus's name.

23. PROMISE: "For when we were yet without strength, in due time Christ died for the ungodly" (Romans 5:6 KJV).

    PRAISE: Savior

PRAYER: Our Father, I pray in Jesus's name that _____ will know You made him/her, and that You will bear, carry, and deliver him/her (Isaiah 46:4).

24. PROMISE: "But where sin abounded, grace did much more abound" (Romans 5:20 KJV).

    PRAISE: Longsuffering

    PRAYER: Our Father, You gave grace to Paul, who said he was "less than the least of all saints" (Ephesians 3:8 KJV). Give _____ grace to do what You created him/her to do. Save _____ in Jesus's name.

25. PROMISE: "That was the true Light which gives light to every man coming into the world" (John 1:9).

    PRAISE: The Lord is the true Light.

    PRAYER: Our Father, cause _____'s lamp, his/her eye, to be good so that his/her whole body is full of light (Matthew 6:22). I pray this in Jesus's name.

26. PROMISE: "For God so loved the world that He gave His only begotten Son, that whoever believes in Him should not perish but have everlasting life" (John 3:16).

    PRAISE: El Olam, Everlasting God

    PRAYER: Our Father, help _____ believe in the Son and have everlasting life. I pray this in Jesus's name.

27. PROMISE: "To Him all the prophets witness that, through His name, whoever believes in Him will receive remission of sins" (Acts 10:43).

PRAISE: Christ, Son of the living God

PRAYER: Our Father, I pray in Jesus's name that _____ will confess that Jesus is "the Christ, the Son of the living God" (Matthew 16:16 KJV).

28. PROMISE: "For whosoever shall call upon the name of the Lord shall be saved" (Romans 10:13 KJV).

PRAISE: Savior

PRAYER: Our Father, I pray _____ will confess You with his/her mouth, believe in his/her heart that You raised Jesus from the dead, and be saved. I pray this in Jesus's name.

29. PROMISE: "I will receive you. I will be a Father to you, And you shall be My sons and daughters, Says the LORD Almighty" (2 Corinthians 6:17–18).

PRAISE: Father

PRAYER: Our Father, I pray _____ will believe in the light and become a son/daughter of light. I pray this in Jesus's name.

30. PROMISE: "And the Spirit and the bride say, 'Come!' And let him who hears say, 'Come!' And let him who thirsts come. Whoever desires, let him take the water of life freely" (Revelation 22:17).

PRAISE: Holy Spirit

PRAYER: Our Father, I pray that _____ will thirst for You, that he/she will desire a relationship with You, and that he/she will take the water of life freely. Call _____, O LORD. I pray in Jesus's name.

31. PROMISE: "So Jesus answered and said to them, 'Have faith in God. For assuredly, I say to you, whoever says to this mountain, "Be removed and be cast into the sea," and does not doubt in his heart, but believes that those things he says will be done, he will have whatever he says'" (Mark 11:22–23).

PRAISE: Omnipotent, all-powerful

PRAYER: Our Father, help _____'s unbelief. I pray this in Jesus's name.

PRAY-ER ENCOURAGEMENT: As Timothy Sturgill once explained in Sunday School, when a Christian says he or she hopes for something, it is different from when a non-believer says it. When non-believers say they hope something will happen, it infers a sense of hopelessness. They really want it but do not believe in it. However, when Christians say they have hope, that hope is rooted in God, His word, and His promises. Optimism and a "confident expectation" are inferred. "But if we hope for that we see not, then do we with patience wait for it" (Romans 8:25 KJV).

WHAT NOW?

Have you ever noticed that storm-clouded sunrises produce magnificent colors? The storm-clouded life can also produce magnificent colors: abundant life, increased faith, more fervent prayer, insights not otherwise possible, a closeness to God, and increased appreciation for blessings.

So, you prayed every prayer in this book. What now?

- If your prodigal is now saved, thank God! Then choose another prodigal for which to pray through the book.
- If your prodigal is not saved but you are seeing raindrops, keep praying until you see complete surrender.
- If you still wait for your prodigal to return to God, keep praying and live your abundant life.

Waiting is difficult, especially when the stakes are so high, but this is how we wait: we wait actively. We pray, we fast, we hold on to the raindrops sent by God to build our faith, we trust God who loves them more than we do and desires they be saved (2 Peter 3:9). We thank Him for all He has already done and all He will do, and we do the next right thing until salvation comes. We do not allow the burden to overtake our lives, and we never stop praying! The wait hasn't changed God or His promises. Instead:

- Walk in victory while praying through circumstances.
- Walk in a faith that repels worry.

- Walk in a faith that allows us to still live the abundant and productive life of God's plan for us, not allowing the situation with our prodigal to cripple us, our life, or our ministry.
- Continue to pray for others and other situations.
- Pray for other prodigals.
- Pray to be the answer to the prayers of another who prays for and loves a prodigal.

Walking in victory and resting in faith does not mean you never feel the Holy Spirit giving you an urgent burden and unction to pray NOW. When that happens, pray fervently until the unction is settled. Then again settle into a rest in the promises of God. We trust. After all, His Word says in 2 Timothy 1:12, "for I know whom I have believed and am persuaded that He is able to keep what I have committed to Him until that Day."

And remember, when the Lord Of Hosts, Jehovah Sabaoth, Commander of the armies of heaven, is with you, you continue to live, continue to go on, and continue to fight, even when the burden is great. Who better to come along with you in this fight than our Almighty God, Jehovah Sabaoth?

"Love suffers long and is kind; love does not envy; love does not parade itself, is not puffed up; does not behave rudely, does not seek its own, is not provoked, thinks no evil; does not rejoice in iniquity, but rejoices in the truth; bears all things, believes all things, hopes all things, endures all things. Love never fails" (1 Corinthians 13:4–8). Because we love them, we never give up.

Believing for them all,

Tami
https://prayer-for-prodigals.com/
https://www.facebook.com/prayerforprodigals7/
https://www.instagram.com/prayerforprodigals7/

APPENDIX A

PROMISES FOR PRAY-ERS

When You Are Fearful

"Fear not, for I am with you; Be not dismayed, for I am your God. I will strengthen you, Yes, I will help you, I will uphold you with My righteous right hand. ... For I, the LORD your God, will hold your right hand, Saying to you, 'Fear not, I will help you'" (Isaiah 41:10, 13).

"Be anxious for nothing, but in everything by prayer and supplication, with thanksgiving, let your requests be made known to God; and the peace of God, which surpasses all understanding, will guard your hearts and minds through Christ Jesus" (Philippians 4:6–7).

(Also read introduction and promises from "January: Do Not Be Afraid.")

When You Are Tired

"Come to Me, all you who labor and are heavy laden, and I will give you rest" (Matthew 11:28).

"He gives power to the weak, And to those who have no might He increases strength" (Isaiah 40:29).

"God is my strength and power, And He makes my way perfect" (2 Samuel 22:33).

"And He said to me, 'My grace is sufficient for you, for My strength is made perfect in weakness'" (2 Corinthians 12:9).

"Therefore my heart is glad, and my glory rejoices; My flesh also will rest in hope" (Psalm 16:9).

"For thus says the Lord GOD, the Holy One of Israel: 'In returning and rest you shall be saved; In quietness and confidence shall be your strength'" (Isaiah 30:15).

When You Don't Know What to Do

Pray:

"Watch and pray, lest you enter into temptation. The spirit indeed is willing, but the flesh is weak" (Matthew 26:41).

"The LORD has heard my supplication; The LORD will receive my prayer" (Psalm 6:9).

"Likewise the Spirit also helps in our weaknesses. For we do not know what we should pray for as we ought, but the Spirit Himself makes intercession for us with groanings which cannot be uttered" (Romans 8:26).

Ask for wisdom:

"If any of you lacks wisdom, let him ask of God, who gives to all liberally and without reproach, and it will be given to him" (James 1:5).

Ask for guidance:

"For You are my rock and my fortress; Therefore, for Your name's sake, Lead me and guide me" (Psalm 31:3).

"I will instruct you and teach you in the way you should go; I will guide you with My eye" (Psalm 32:8).

Trust God:

"It is better to trust in the LORD than to put confidence in man" (Psalm 118:8 KJV).

"Trust in the LORD with all your heart, And lean not on your own understanding; In all your ways acknowledge Him, And He shall direct your paths" (Proverbs 3:5–6).

"God is our refuge and strength, a very present help in trouble" (Psalm 46:1 KJV).

Think on appropriate things:
"Finally, brethren, whatsoever things are true, whatsoever things are honest, whatsoever things are just, whatsoever things are pure, whatsoever things are lovely, whatsoever things are of good report; if there be any virtue, and if there be any praise, think on these things" (Philippians 4:8 KJV).

"You will keep him in perfect peace, Whose mind is stayed on You, Because he trusts in You" (Isaiah 26:3).

Give thanks:
"In every thing give thanks: for this is the will of God in Christ Jesus concerning you" (1 Thessalonians 5:18 KJV).

Praise:
Praise the LORD! "Praise Him for His mighty acts; praise Him according to His excellent greatness! ... Let everything that has breath praise the LORD" (Psalm 150:2, 6).

"The LORD is my strength and song, And He has become my salvation; He is my God, and I will praise Him. ... Your right hand, O LORD, has become glorious in power; Your right hand, O LORD, has dashed the enemy in pieces. And in the greatness of Your excellence You have overthrown those who rose against You. ... Who is like You, O LORD, among the gods? Who is like You, glorious in holiness, Fearful in praises, doing wonders?" (Exodus 15:2, 6–7, 11).

Listen:
"Your ears shall hear a word behind you, saying, 'This is the way, walk in it,' Whenever you turn to the right hand Or whenever you turn to the left" (Isaiah 30:21).

"I will instruct you and teach you in the way should go; I will guide you with My eye" (Psalm 32:8).

Do the next right thing:
"Not slothful in business; fervent in spirit; serving the Lord; Rejoicing in hope; patient in tribulation; continuing instant in prayer;

Distributing to the necessity of saints; given to hospitality" (Romans 12:11–13 KJV).

"Rejoice evermore. Pray without ceasing. In every thing give thanks: for this is the will of God in Christ Jesus concerning you" (1 Thessalonians 5:16–18 KJV).

"And let us not be weary in well doing: for in due season we shall reap, if we faint not" (Galatians 6:9 KJV).

"Therefore, my beloved brethren, be steadfast, immovable, always abounding in the work of the Lord, knowing that your labor is not in vain in the Lord" (1 Corinthians 15:58).

Get up, brush your teeth, shower, fix food, laundry, go to work, clean the house, mow the lawn, work on your ministry, answer your calling, and fulfill your purpose.

Wait on the Lord:
"Wait on the LORD; Be of good courage, And He shall strengthen your heart; Wait, I say, on the LORD!" (Psalm 27:14).

"Draw nigh to God, and he will draw nigh to you" (James 4:8 KJV).

When You Don't Know Where Your Prodigal Is, God Does

"Where can I go from Your Spirit? Or where can I flee from Your presence? If I ascend into heaven, You are there; if I make my bed in hell, behold, You are there" (Psalm 139:7–8).

"For He Himself has said, 'I will never leave you nor forsake you'" (Hebrews 13:5).

"'Can anyone hide himself in secret places, So I shall not see him?' says the LORD; 'Do I not fill heaven and earth?'" (Jeremiah 23:24).

When Your Faith Is Challenged

(Read the introduction and promises for "July: He is Faithful")

When You Need Boldness in Prayer

"Let us therefore come boldly unto the throne of grace, that we may obtain mercy, and find grace to help in time of need" (Hebrews 4:16 KJV).

"Then, behold, the veil of the temple was torn in two from top to bottom; and the earth quaked, and the rocks were split" (Matthew 27:51). We have direct access to the presence of God.

"Therefore, brethren, having boldness to enter the Holiest by the blood of Jesus, by a new and living way which He consecrated for us, through the veil, that is, His flesh, and having a High Priest over the house of God, let us draw near with a true heart in full assurance of faith." (Hebrews 10:19–22).

"casting all your care upon Him, for He cares for you" (1 Peter 5:7).

APPENDIX B

PRAYERS FOR CERTAIN CIRCUMSTANCES WITH YOUR PRODIGAL

A Prayer for EVERY DAY

PROMISE: "To open the blind eyes, to bring out the prisoners from the prison, and them that sit in darkness out of the prison house" (Isaiah 42:7 KJV).

PRAISE: Father

PRAYER: Our Father, You are able, so please "do exceedingly abundantly above all that we ask or think" in _____ 's life, "according to [Your] power that works in us" (Ephesians 3:20). Open his/her eyes so he/she can see You and his/her ears so he/she can hear. Open his/her mind so he/she can know You and his/her heart to receive what You have for him/her. Deliver _____ from evil. In Jesus's name I pray.

Prayer for RESTORATION

PROMISE: "God, who gives life to the dead and calls those things which do not exist as though they did" (Romans 4:17).

PRAISE: Redeemer

PRAYER: Our Father, I pray _____, who is "alienated and enemies in [his/her] mind by wicked works," would be reconciled to You (Colossians 1:21 KJV). Cause Your kingdom to come to our family, to _____. You have a purpose for him/her, but Satan is robbing him/her of this time with You; save him/her and restore to him/her and to Your kingdom those things lost, and doubly anoint him/her for work in Your kingdom.

　　Thank You for the comfort, beauty, joy, and praise that You are working from these circumstances. _____ has gone on "backsliding in the way of his heart," so look on his/her ways, and heal; guide him/her and comfort those who mourn for him/her (Isaiah 57:17-18). Save him/her and restore the years that the locust has eaten; pour out Your Spirit on _____ (Joel 2:25, 28).

　　Jesus, thank you for dying for _____.

　　Our Father, in Jesus's name I pray.

Prayer for SALVATION

PROMISE: "For God sent not His Son into the world to condemn the world; but that the world through him might be saved" (John 3:17 KJV).

PRAISE: Savior

PRAYER: Our Father, although You do not force anyone to be saved, we pray according to Your word that You will set _____ up to receive salvation: send laborers into his/her harvest field (Matthew 9:38), replace ungodly influence with godly (Psalm 1:1), remove his/her heart of stone and give him/her a heart of flesh (Ezekiel 11:19), convict him/her of sin (John 16:8), draw him/her to Yourself (John 6:44), and give him/her a godly sorrow that will lead to repentance—a repentance that will lead to salvation (2 Corinthians 7:9–10). Set _____ up.

　　"O Lord, hear! O Lord, forgive! O Lord, listen and act! Do not delay for Your own sake, my God" (Daniel 9:19). Do not look at _____'s sins, and erase all his/her iniquities (Psalm 51:9). Show your mercy to him/her. Yes, he/she has sinned, but Your Word says your mercies and compassions are new every morning (Lamentations 3:22–23). I pray nothing will hinder his/her coming to You (Matthew 19:14). Keep him/her from doing anything that will hinder his/her salvation and calling, ministry, and purpose. Protect his/her mind, body, soul, and spirit.

Cause _____ to "lay aside every weight, and the sin which so easily ensnares" him/her (Hebrews 12:1). Father, please, remove every obstacle in his/her path on his/her way back to You. I pray _____ will call on Your name and be saved. In Jesus's name I pray.

If Your Prodigal's FAITH IS WEAK

PROMISE: "God has dealt to each one a measure of faith" (Romans 12:3).

PRAISE: Author and Finisher of faith

PRAYER: Our Father, thank You for the measure of faith You have given _____. I pray his/her faith will take root and grow into salvation, and continue to grow exceedingly (2 Thessalonians 1:3). I pray his/her faith would not be in the wisdom of men, but that he/she will trust in Your power (1 Corinthians 2:5).

Your word says that "faith comes by hearing, and hearing by the word of God" (Romans 10:17). _____ has known the Holy Scriptures from childhood, and I ask they will make him/her "wise unto salvation through faith which is in Christ Jesus" (2 Timothy 3:15 KJV).

Father, You helped doubting Thomas, meeting him where his doubt was and revealing Yourself in a way that built his faith (John 20:27). Meet _____ and reveal Yourself in a way that builds his/her faith and restores him/her to salvation.

Father, Satan desires to sift _____ as wheat, but I pray that the faith You have given to him/her will not fail (Luke 22:31–32). Instead, I pray he/she will look unto Jesus, Your Son, the author and finisher of faith (Hebrews 12:2). In Jesus's name I pray.

If Your Prodigal NEEDS HOPE for Salvation; If Your Prodigal Believes He Cannot be Saved

PROMISE: "If we confess our sins, he is faithful and just to forgive us our sins, and to cleanse us from all unrighteousness" (1 John 1:9 KJV). "The Lord is not slack concerning his promise, as some men count slackness; but is longsuffering to us-ward, not willing that any should perish, but that all should come to repentance" (2 Peter 3:9 KJV).

PRAISE: Savior

PRAYER: Our Father, I pray _____ will know that nothing is too hard for You, will have hope in You, and will say that You are his/her portion (Lamentations 3:24). Your word promises thoughts of peace and not for evil; please, give him/her the future for which You created him/her, and give hope in You (Jeremiah 29:11). Cause him/her to know he/she can be redeemed and forgiven and cause him/her to call on You for salvation and say, "God be merciful to me a sinner!" (Luke 18:13 KJV). Enlighten _____'s eyes of understanding to know the hope that comes with being called by Christ and Your exceedingly great power toward believers (Ephesians 1:18–19). In Jesus's name I pray.

If Your Prodigal is DECEIVED

PROMISE: "For the LORD is good; His mercy is everlasting, And His truth endures to all generations" (Psalm 100:5).

PRAISE: Truth

PRAYER: Our Father, _____ has been taught about You from his/her youth but is deceived (Psalm 71:17). I pray every lie Satan has told him/her will be exposed and that Your truth will prevail, because the truth shall make him/her free (John 8:32). I pray the devil will not be allowed to take the Word out of his/her heart, so he/she can believe and be saved (Luke 8:12). I pray _____ will not allow himself/herself to be deceived by spirits and demon's doctrines, speak hypocritical lies, or have his/her "conscience seared with a hot iron" (1 Timothy 4:1–2 KJV). I ask that _____ no longer "be conformed to this world, but be transformed by the renewing of [his/her] mind" (Romans 12:2). Cause him/her to no longer walk in the futility of his/her mind, no longer have his/her understanding darkened, and no longer be alienated from the life of God (Ephesians 4:17–18). Help those around him/her to use the mighty weapons in You to pull down strongholds in his/her life, "casting down arguments and every high thing that exalts itself against the knowledge of [You], bringing every thought into captivity to the obedience of [You]" (2 Corinthians 10:5).

I pray _____ will no longer be childish, "tossed to and fro, and carried about with every wind of doctrine, by the sleight of men, and cunning craftiness, whereby they lie in wait to deceive" (Ephesians 4:14 KJV). I pray he/she will "Beware lest any man spoil [him/her] through philosophy and vain deceit, after the tradition of men, after the rudiments of the world, and not after Christ" (Colossians 2:8 KJV). Father, help him/her to see that the wisdom of the age in Your Word is infinitely superior to the so-called wisdom of New Age philosophies. I also pray against the lies of evolution. I pray he/she will know that YOU created him/her, and that he/she is not a product of evolution. Father, bless _____'s eyes so he/she can see You and his/her ears so he/she can hear You (Matthew 13:16). In Jesus's name I pray.

If Your Prodigal DOESN'T BELIEVE

PROMISE: "If we are faithless, He remains faithful; He cannot deny Himself" (2 Timothy 2:13).

PRAISE: Faithful

PRAYER: Our Father, thank You for the reminder that even when we do not have faith, You are still faithful; unbelief doesn't change who You are. _____ says he/she does not believe in You. Satan has blinded _____ so that he/she cannot see the light of the gospel. You are the God who commanded light to shine out of darkness. Please, shine Your light in _____ 's heart so he/she will have knowledge of Your glory and see You again (2 Corinthians 4:4, 6). The gospel has been veiled from his/her mind, and his/her mind has been blinded to keep him from believing. Lift the veil, I pray. Help his/her unbelief. Cause him/her to KNOW Jesus is THE way, THE truth, THE life (John 14:6), and not just a possibility or just a good man. I pray _____ will believe that Jesus is the Son of God so he/she can overcome the world (1 John 5:4–5) and believe in his/her heart that You raised Jesus from the dead and be saved (Romans 10:9). In Jesus's name I pray.

If Your Prodigal's Life Is Full of UNGODLY INFLUENCES

PROMISE: "The LORD brings the counsel of the nations to nothing; He makes the plans of the peoples of no effect. The counsel of the LORD stands forever, the plans of His heart to all generations" (Psalm 33:10–11).

PRAISE: Jehovah Raah, The Lord Our Shepherd

PRAYER: Our Father, we are fighting for _____ through prayer, as You have required. He/she spends time with people who can be bad influences. Instead, cause him/her to walk not in the counsel of the ungodly but the godly, nor stand in the path of sinners but the righteous, nor sit in the seat of the scornful but the joyful. Let his/her delight be in Your law, and cause him/her to meditate in it day and night (Psalm 1:1–2).

I pray _____ will choose his/her friends carefully so that the way of the wicked will not lead him/her astray (Proverbs 12:26). I pray that he/she will "Beware of false prophets, which come … in sheep's clothing, but inwardly they are ravening wolves" (Matthew 7:15 KJV), and that You will cause the counsel of the nations and people's plans to have no effect in his/her life, and Your counsel and plans to stand forever for him/her and all of his/her descendants.

Father, _____ did run well, but someone hindered him/her so that he/she "should not obey the truth" (Galatians 5:7 KJV). Cause the love of godly people around him/her to be without hypocrisy (Romans

12:9). You sent Peter to the house of Cornelius. Send someone to witness to _____ to move him/her to salvation (Acts 10). Send laborers into the harvest field that is _____'s life. I pray this in Jesus's name.

If You See Raindrops in the Life of Your Prodigal, But He/She Is NOT TOTALLY SURRENDERED

PROMISE: "being confident of this very thing, that He who has begun a good work in you will complete it until the day of Jesus Christ" (Philippians 1:6).

PRAISE: Sovereign; Savior; Shepherd

PRAYER: Our Father, thank You for all you have already done to bring _____ back to Yourself. I am confident of this very thing, that You have begun a good work in him/her in answer to my prayers, and I thank You for working when I can see and when I cannot. I ask that You will complete that work until the day of Christ. He/she walks in trouble, so I pray You will revive and save him/her, come against his/her enemies, and "perfect that which concerns [him/her]. … Do not forsake the works of Your hands" (Psalm 138:7–8). Make him/her "perfect, thoroughly furnished unto all good works" (2 Timothy 3:17 KJV), complete in You, "the head of all principality and power" (Colossians 2:10 KJV). I pray he/she will be brought back from captivity like You did Zion. You have already done great things for him/her. Cause him/her to remember them and shout joyfully to You, gladly serve You, and sing in Your presence. Jesus, save _____ to the uttermost. Thank You for always making intercession for him/her. In Jesus's name I pray.

If Your Prodigal is MAKING BAD CHOICES

PROMISE: "For I will not contend forever, Nor will I always be angry; For the spirit would fail before Me, And the souls which I have made.

For the iniquity of his covetousness I was angry and struck him; I hid and was angry, And he went on backsliding in the way of his heart. I have seen his ways, and will heal him; I will also lead him, and restore comforts to him And to his mourners" (Isaiah 57:16–18).

PRAISE: The Way

PRAYER: Our Father, _____ is making bad decisions. I pray he/she will submit to You, resist the devil so he will flee, draw near to You so You will draw near to him/her, cleanse his/her hands, and purify his/her heart (James 4:7–8). I pray You will redeem his/her life from destruction, forgive him/her of all iniquities, and crown him/her with lovingkindness and tender mercies (Psalm 103:3–4). When _____ seeks sin, do not let him/her find it. As you promised to do for Hosea, build a hedge and make a wall around _____ so he/she cannot find the way to sinful places. Cause him/her to say, "I will go and return to [the Lord]; for then was it better with me than now" (Hosea 2:6–7 KJV). _____ has chosen a path that is destroying him/her. I pray that You will cause him/her to ponder the path of his/her feet and establish all of his/her ways, that he/she will turn not to the right or the left and will remove his/her foot from evil (Proverbs 4:26–27). If he/she decides to turn to the right or left, cause him/her to hear You speaking, telling him/her which way he/she should walk (Isaiah 30:21). I pray when _____ is tempted to sin, that he/she will find the way of escape and take it (1 Corinthians 10:13) and will present his/her body "a living sacrifice, holy, acceptable unto [You], which is [his/her] reasonable service" (Romans 12:1 KJV). I pray he/she will "Depart from evil, and do good; seek peace, and pursue it" (Psalm 34:14 KJV). Cause him/her to abhor evil things and to cling to good things. (Romans 12:9). In Jesus's name I pray.

If Your Prodigal is ADDICTED

PROMISE: "The Spirit of the Lord GOD is upon Me, Because the LORD has anointed Me To preach good tidings to the poor; He has sent Me to heal the brokenhearted, To proclaim liberty to the captives, And the opening of the prison to those who are bound" (Regarding the Son in Isaiah 61:1).

PRAISE: El, God Of Power And Might; omnipotent, all-powerful God; Savior

PRAYER: Our Father, _____ has been taken captive by Satan and is bound by addiction. Bring him/her out of darkness and the shadow of death, and break his/her chains in pieces. Break "the gates of brass, and cut the bars of iron in sunder" (Psalm 107:14, 16 KJV). Proclaim liberty to him/her and open his/her prison doors. Make him/her no longer be a slave but a son/daughter and Your heir (Galatians 4:7). Cause him/her to firmly stay in the freedom You will give (Galatians 5:1). Bring him/her up out the horrible pit and miry clay that he/she is in; set his/her feet on a rock, and establish his/her steps; put a new song in his/her mouth (Psalm 40:2–3). I pray _____ will recover out of the snare of the devil, who has taken him/her captive to do his will (2 Timothy 2:26). In Jesus's name I pray.

If Your Prodigal is IN A DARK PLACE

PROMISE: "He has delivered us from the power of darkness and conveyed us into the kingdom of the Son of His love, in whom we have redemption through His blood, the forgiveness of sins" (Colossians 1:13–14).

PRAISE: Light

PRAYER: Our Father, deliver _____ from the power of darkness and translate him/her into Your Son's kingdom. I pray _____'s eyes will be opened so he/she will be turned to light from darkness and to God instead of being controlled by Satan's power, so his/her sins can be forgiven and he/she can be sanctified by faith in You (Acts 26:18).

God, Your word promises it will stand forever (Isaiah 40:8). I am believing Your word which _____ has heard, read, and memorized will stand, and I am asking that Your word will light the path back to You. I pray You will seek him/her out and deliver him/her from all the places the enemy has taken him/her in the darkness. I pray _____, who is walking in darkness and dwells in the shadow of death, will see a great light (Isaiah 9:2–3). Increase his/her joy and cause him/her to rejoice before You.

At creation You spoke, and there was light. I pray You will say for _____, "Let there be light" (Genesis 1:3 KJV). Awaken him/her who is sleeping spiritually; raise him/her from the dead, and give him/her light (Ephesians 5:14). In Jesus's name I pray.

MY RAINDROPS

These pages are a good place to document answers—both large and small—to your prayers, along with the dates. When you need to remember that God is working, come back to this page, give thanks for prayers already answered, claim the promise from Philippians 1:6 that says, "being confident of this very thing, that He who has begun a good work in you will complete it until the day of Jesus Christ," and ask God to help your unbelief. If you would like to read more about Raindrops, check the introduction to the month of April.

_____

_____

_____

_____

_____

_____

_____

_____

_____

_____

_____

_____

Tami Winkelman

MY RAINDROPS

MY RAINDROPS

Tami Winkelman

MY RAINDROPS

ABOUT THE AUTHOR

Tami Winkelman is the founder of Prayer for Prodigals, a ministry with global reach. She knows first-hand the ups and downs of prayerfully loving a prodigal and is passionate about helping others to pray and rest in God's promises until their prodigals come back to God. She and her husband Kevin have been married for over 36 years and have two amazing grown children and one magnificently brilliant grandson.

76741107R00117

Made in the USA
Columbia, SC
26 September 2019